FRAGMENTS, WINDOWS AND OTHER PLAYS

By Murray Schisgal

THE TYPISTS AND THE TIGER
LUV
FRAGMENTS, WINDOWS AND OTHER PLAYS

Murray Schisgal

FRAGMENTS, WINDOWS
and
OTHER PLAYS

WITH AN INTRODUCTION BY M. J. ARLEN

Coward-McCann, Inc.
New York

Library of Congress Catalog Card Number: 65-20403

To Diane, Julie, Stephen
Renée & Mark Troy

CONTENTS

MURRAY SCHISGAL:

PORTRAIT OF THE PLAYWRIGHT
IN THE CATBIRD SEAT

by M. J. Arlen

Luv, as nearly everyone must know by now, is the swell new play of the season—funny, truly very funny, fresh, alive, intelligent and filled with a kind of human warmth one rarely sees in plays, or in anything else for that matter—and its author is Murray Schisgal (accent on the last syllable. That's it. Murray Schisgal), who, at the semiadvanced age of 37, at a stage in life when Truman Capote had already published his Collected Works and Leonard Bernstein had been on the cover of The Saturday Review 72 times, is having his first real, tangible, certified, public success.

And a very large success it is, too. Luv is not only a smash hit in the traditional sense, meaning that the friendly, wizened

9]

ticket agent in the lobby of the O'Selznick Hotel cannot get you in to see it next Saturday night, that *The New York Times* has been running the usual quota of descriptive notes about the line outside the box office (the *Times* has described the line, variously, as "sinuous" and "winding," also traditional) and that Schisgal stands to make a bundle of boodle from the enterprise. It is also, oh rare and marvelous event, a super critical hit, which means that the critics to a man, even the meanest and nastiest of critics, the critics who break a grown man's reputation with a snap of their fingers, who can plunge cities into darkness, whole continents into war, etc. (you know perfectly well which critics I mean), have written about *Luv* with an unreserved and gladsome enthusiasm seldom found outside the prose of stockbrokers on the financial page. Walter Kerr, for example, has called *Luv* "the answer to a theatre-goer's prayer," and recently began a piece for his paper with the sentence, "I am going to write 900 words on why I like Murray Schisgal."

The recipient of all this adulation, affection, applause and critical hymn-singing ("For the precious boon of laughter, much thanks . . . ," Howard Taubman. *Howard Taubman?*) is a stoutish—no, let us be honest—stout, affable, intelligent, hard-working, unaffected, somewhat rumpled figure, who regards his recent, speedy escalation to the position of one of America's foremost and best and hottest playwrights with the sober wariness of a man who discovers that his bank has just made a sizable bookkeeping error in his favor. "Success!" says Schisgal. "People think as soon as you have success you want to go out and change your life. For example, everybody right now wants me to do musical comedies. Why should I all of a sudden want to do musical comedies? I'm tone deaf. Eight

[10

months ago, of course, when I didn't have too much money, I don't remember so many people wanting me to do a musical comedy. Eight months ago, if anybody had asked me to, I'd have probably gotten on the stage and danced."

Eight months ago! Not too much money! Talk about your American dream! Talk about your land of opportunity, wherein a young man of talent, industry and ambition may rise within the twinkling of an eye (in this instance, a 16- or 17-year twinkling) from the job of dress hanger-upper in Klein's Department Store to that of nationally and internationally renowned playwright ("Playwright Schisgal devastates our pious obsessions in a holocaust of laughter," *Time*), justly admired for his dramatic gifts and in hot demand for musicomedy adaptations. Actually, eight months ago things were probably not too bad for Schisgal because *Luv*, at any rate, was in rehearsal—but he has not for long been in the catbird seat, or in fact anywhere near it.

Schisgal is a New Yorker. He has been a New Yorker since birth—his father was a clothes-presser across the river in Brooklyn. He has been a serious writer since he was 19 or 20. "There wasn't much money," he says. "I did odd jobs all over the place, because I needed to live, of course, and because I wanted something that would give me time in which to write." On various occasions he has set pins in a bowling alley, played in a band, pushed hand trucks in the garment district and, oh yes, once worked as a dress hanger-upper in Klein's Department Store. In the meantime, he went to college at night. He even went to Brooklyn Law School, obtained a law degree and became a lawyer. "I thought I ought to have something else going for me, and that I might as well be a lawyer. But it took too much time from my writing, and too much attention."

11]

Schisgal worked in a law office for two years down on Delancey Street and then quit—to teach school.

He continued to write all the time. "After all, if you're a writer, what else are you going to do? In those days I wrote stories and novels. Three novels. They really weren't much good, or at least nobody thought they were good enough to publish. I used to send the stories—there must have been about 60 of them—to little magazines like *Epic*. I sent the novels everywhere, the usual places. Then, around three years ago, I was teaching English at the James Fenimore Cooper Junior High School in East Harlem and starting in on my fourth novel, when I decided to turn to playwriting. No, it wasn't brought about by any particular plan. The novel was going badly. I was stuck, and so I thought I'd try another form. After all, if you're a writer, you don't exclude any form, do you? You just write. If the plays hadn't worked out, I'd probably be writing essays now."

Schisgal wrote five one-act plays as an East Harlem schoolteacher, then left his job and, with the plays as yet unproduced, took off for Spain to do more writing. On his way through London, at a friend's suggestion, he dropped the five plays off at the British Drama League, and before he'd gotten out of town the Drama League called and offered to produce two of them, *The Typists* and *The Tiger*. Since that happy experience, Schisgal has felt warmly about the European theatre, and Europeans have felt warmly about him, having translated and performed his plays, to date, in at least a dozen languages.

A year later, *The Typist* and *The Tiger* were done off-Broadway with Eli Wallach and Anne Jackson in the cast (*as* the cast). They were very well received, won two awards—the Vernon Rice and the Outer Circle—even earned a little money and placed Schisgal squarely on the scene as a truly good, serious and funny playwright. The next year, he had another play put on in London, this time a full-length job called *Ducks and Lovers*, which will be produced in New York, possibly this fall; and one in Boston (for Bostonians), called *Knit One, Purl Two*. And, in November of 1964, *Luv* opened at the Booth Theatre in New York, a three-character play directed by Mike Nichols, with Eli Wallach, Anne Jackson and Alan Arkin as the three characters. And Murray Schisgal had finally arrived.

Murray Schisgal sits at home on his new couch in his new living room. It is a smallish, attractive, sunlit room—a few chairs, a coffee table, a small bookcase hanging on the wall—with a view to the left, across the roofs of brownstone houses, to the Hudson River, and, to the right, of a small dining area, where his wife is giving their year-old daughter lunch. He wears a pair of rumpled khaki trousers, a blue-checked short-sleeved sports shirt, a white T-shirt, a pair of floppy shoes and a beard. The beard is neither small nor large. How to describe it? As beards go, it is somewhat between William Howard Taft's and Dwight MacDonald's. Schisgal has a whitish face, at least in early spring he had a whitish face, and what with the beard, and the dark eyebrows, and the vaguely sad look (*The New York Times* man noticed this too, so possibly it is just a result of being interviewed), the effect is powerfully rabbinical.

He is working right now on two plays. One of them is brand-new. *Jimmy Shine*. The other is *Ducks and Lovers*, which he is rewriting for the American production. "I love to rewrite," he said. "I'm addicted to it. If I didn't have someone pressing me, I could rewrite endlessly, *forever*, and without changing anything much." He works at present in a small, tele-

13]

phoneless hotel room three blocks away, which is one of his few indulgences since coming into money—the other indulgences being the apartment (he has moved his family from a three-room apartment at 98th and West End Avenue to a five-room apartment at 101st and West End Avenue) and getting his teeth fixed. He also has plans to buy a new hat. "I saw a velour hat on Fifth Avenue the other day," he says.

What about the meaning of *Luv?* he was asked. Nearly everyone who sees it says it is very funny and *deep* and turns the preoccupations-of-modern-life upside-down, but some of the people are perplexed and pettish because they feel they ought to know *exactly* what it is about, and they aren't sure. Schisgal clasps his hands together and appears, briefly, to be praying into them. He unclasps his hands and looks at the floor. He looks at the coffee table. He clasps his hands together again and prays some more. "I don't know why it is," he says, "that people always seem to want everything tied up for them in a neat little bundle—a story they can put their fingers on and say, look, here's the story. For my part, I don't see why it has to be that way. I think of the theatre as an experience. What takes place on stage is an experience, and the audience is a part of it."

He took some coffee. "That's very important to me," he went on. "I don't write my plays in a vacuum. I write them for an audience. And, for me, the great thing about *Luv* has been that so many people, apparently, have been affected by it. You see, the performing of a play is a very special kind of activity. It's a communal activity, really. If you look back at the theatre, the great theatre, the Elizabethans, the Greeks, you see that there's always been a strong state of tension and—well, empathy, between the audience and the play. And without this state of tension, you have no true sense of theatre, of what theatre can be. You have no theatre. Besides," he said, "I don't think people go to the theatre for—answers. They go for the whole experience."

Schisgal, at present, is at an interesting (for us) and (for him) a doubtless strange and exciting moment in his career. He is no young puppy. He is not *old*, to be sure. Who thinks anyone under 57 is *old*? But he is 37, and, at 37, he stands on the threshold of what could very well be a most considerable and significant career in the American theatre. And if that sounds portentous in print, consider how it must seem to Schisgal, who has to do the threshold-standing. To date, there is no doubt that he has done some very good work. *Luv*, in fact, is very likely a "classic," a funny *serious* play which says more about Love, Money, Sex Guilt, Freud—the whole great panoply of (if you will pardon the expression) The Modern Predicament—than the last 92 pretentious, complacent, rhetorical Modern Dramas rolled into one. And how far can he go? Well, it would be downright silly to try to say. Schisgal is a very genuine talent, a serious man. He will go as far as he can, and nobody, not even he, can know how far that really is.

"I can't say that the success of *Luv* makes it any easier to do the next play," he says. "Of course, it makes some things easier. It's really pretty nice by now to be making good money. I haven't spent a lot of it, actually I haven't received a lot of it yet. But it's nice to know that you can write for the next couple of years without having to worry about taking another job."

And what about his writing? Does he plan to continue in the same vein? Two- or three-character plays, for instance? "Well, *Jimmy Shine*," he says, "has 27 characters, which should give

15]

you some idea. You know, I think there are perhaps a handful of American playwrights who are experienced enough to know the direction of their own work, and I can't say that I count myself among them. I have no general rules about playwriting and so each time I sit down at the typewriter it's a new experience for me. But you take somebody who's older and has been working at it longer. Ionesco, for example, or Samuel Beckett. I think it's fairly accurate to say that so far they've pursued a single style. And the slightly younger men, Tennessee Williams and Miller. They've probably also found their final dramatic voices by now, in that you don't see too much fundamental change in their work. But in my case, well I don't know what my dramatic voice is, and I don't know that I ever will. I'm not at all sure that it's either necessary or desirable to do so."

Schisgal seems very much his own man. He also seems very much a writer, rather than a literary man. He talks easily and unaffectedly, slowly for the most part, and without the verve of the practiced, or practicing, conversationalist. Somebody once observed that very few really good writers are good talkers, and although there are exceptions to this the generality is probably as true as most.

He is keen to acknowledge his satisfaction at the way *Luv* was put on the stage at the Booth. "It was a good experience," he says. "From start to finish, a good experience. People, you know, ask me questions about how much of the funny stuff in *Luv* is Mike Nichols' work, and how much of it is mine, and although I tend to answer rather automatically now that the contribution of the director and actors equaled my own, that is exactly the way I think it was. Everybody involved made constructive contributions.

[16

"You know," he continued, "you hear so many *negative* things about the Broadway theatre, about all the pressures, and the conniving, and the prostitution of some poor joker's artistic integrity, and I'm sure it's true, I'm sure it happens— but I've just never happened to have found any of it myself. In the case of *Luv*, the people got the script, and said they wanted to do it, and that was that. No pressures. Nobody once asked me to compromise. In the entire course of the production I was never once made aware of the usual things people have complained about in the Broadway theatre."

And, each evening now, at the Booth Theatre, the "Standing Room Only" hangs primly from the box-office grille, the limousines line up outside, and the audience, surely the same audience which sits glassily through all those poetry readings, and coughs throughout the mad scene in *Lear*, and produces that eerie, joyless, campfire laughter at any of the 15 new comedies in town—this audience literally unfolds itself in pleasure and—well, empathy. Some nights, say people who tend the back of the house, the laughter never really stops— the enjoyment—what Schisgal speaks of as this participation between the audience and the play and players.

It is a splendid thing to witness, not just the play, but the response as well. It is a kind of rapport, the wise men say, which you get only in the theatre (and how often do you get it there?). And does Schisgal himself come by, come by just now and then, to watch the show and feel the laughter? "No, no," he says. He shakes his head. "It's much too much like visiting the dead. All those happy, happy memories. Besides, I'm doing other work right now."

FRAGMENTS

FRAGMENTS

SCENE:

A room divided into three smaller "rooms" only by the arrangement of the furniture which is asymmetrical yet well-defined. JAX's *"room" is almost bare: a cot and a pair of crutches that lean against the wall.* BAXTER's *is cluttered, disorderly: piles of dirty clothes are all about.* MAX's *is cleanly and sensibly furnished with, among other things, a large desk on which there are papers, books, portfolios, etc.*

The three young men who share the room are of approximately equal height and if possible of similar color and feature. MAX's *posture and bearing are those of a soldier; his hair is trimmed in a crew cut.* BAXTER *tends to a flatulent pudginess.* JAX *is gaunt; a scraggly neglected beard hangs from his sickly face.*

The curtain rises on JAX *who is lying on his cot, supine, covered to his ankles with blankets; his shoes protrude, pointing upward. His eyes are fixed habitually on the ceiling. He breathes heavily, speaks in a deep hoarse unnatural voice, with great effort, with seemingly the last of his strength. He now cries out:* "Oh, my God." *He then laughs mockingly at his own agonized invocation. Then:* "It's over. At last . . . It's over.

Come, now, now, now, now . . ." His body seems to stiffen. He is silent.

In a moment BAXTER *enters. His clothes are rumpled, disheveled, his hair uncombed, his skin grimy, unwashed.*

BAXTER. Jax? Jax, I'm back. Don't ask me where I was. Don't ask me. I don't know. I don't know what happened to me.
Picks up toy telescope, squints through it at room across alleyway.
Is she in tonight? How'd she look? The light's on. She has to be in. I don't see her, though.
He removes his jacket and changes his shirt, socks and shoes, picking them up from the floor; they are no improvement over the clothes he has taken off.
What a nightmare. How long was I gone? Four days? A week? I don't know what the hell's got into me. I remember walking down to Second Avenue, to the grocer's. I told you I was only going down for a bottle of milk; that's all I had in mind. You know I'm telling you the truth. But . . . In the street . . . Did I see anything? What was it? I don't remember. Some dirty kids playing in the gutter, yelling . . . A car, a big yellow convertible it was, with an old man sitting behind the wheel, honking the horn . . . A woman, there was a woman sitting on a stoop, one hand across her lap, the other hand was holding her chin; her eyes . . . No. That wasn't it. I don't remember, Jax. But I . . . I went up to Third Avenue and I had a beer. I had

a beer and . . . I don't remember. Jax? Jax, are you all right? Is anything wrong? Jax?

> *He moves toward him, about to cross invisible line into his "room."*

JAX. (*Without looking at him*) Don't come into my room.

BAXTER. I wasn't. I wasn't, Jax. I thought something might have been wrong. Jax, I did some terrible things, some awful things. I didn't want to start drinking. That wasn't what I had in mind. I was going down for a bottle of milk. Don't you remember me telling you, "I'll be back in five minutes, Jax. Five minutes." And I meant it. I wasn't lying. I went down. It was beautiful out. I never saw the sky looking so blue, so real, not in the city; the air was nice and warm, and the trees in the churchyard, they were out in leaves . . . I didn't want to start drinking, Jax. Do you believe me? Do you believe me, Jax?

> *No answer; angrily.*

Are you deaf? Is today your day to be deaf?

> *He starts toward* JAX's *"room."*

JAX. (*Without looking at him*) Don't come into my room.

BAXTER. I thought so. Jax, you are the biggest phony this side of hell. Do you hear me? You're a phony, buddy, a phony, a hypocrite, a liar, a stinking rotting skeleton . . .

> *He stops suddenly; sits down, brushes back his hair.*

I don't know why I bother talking to you. If you knew some of the things I did these past few days . . . I'm worse than you are. I'm worse. What the hell got into me? Why did I start drinking? And . . . Why did I stop? Jax . . . Jax, I can't live in this world. I can't. I always want to cry, did you know that? My head is filled with tears, it's bloated and swollen with tears. They drown my eyes, my tongue; when I cut my face shaving in the morning they pour out like a cataract; and when I . . . Ahh, what's the use. It's no good. I don't want to be any good, do I? Can I? Will I? Jax, do you have any money? Jax . . . Please . . . You bastard! You selfish bastard!

He puts telescope to his eye.

She's there now. There she is. She was taking a shower. She's wearing her terry-cloth bathrobe. I can almost smell the soap and steam rising from her body. Ohh, she's nice, Jax. She's really nice. If I had a woman like that . . . I'd say, "I love. I love you. I love you." Wouldn't it be something to say, "I love you?" To actually say it, out loud?

Abruptly.

I need a drink. There's no getting away from it. I've got to have a drink and that's a fact of life.

Hesitating, then stepping into MAX's *"room" where he searches about for money.*

Lucky for me you can't see what I'm doing. You've been blind for a week, haven't you, Jax? How are your legs? Still paralyzed? Poor poor Jax. They're giving you a rough time, aren't they?

JAX. Write a letter for me.

BAXTER. Go to hell.

JAX. I'm dying, Baxter.

BAXTER. If you weren't I wouldn't recognize you.

JAX. One letter. One last letter. Then you can divide the room in half. More room for you, more room for him.

BAXTER. That I'd like. Maybe it wouldn't be so bad then. But how do I know you're telling the truth? You've said all this before, buddy. What guarantees do you give me?

JAX. My willpower, the last of my strength, the last of my convictions.

BAXTER. (*With interest*) You're going to force yourself . . .

JAX. I have nothing to do with it.

BAXTER. I've never seen a dead person, Jax. I want you to die. I want to see you dead. When you die, Jax, I'm going to celebrate. That's right. I'm going to dance in the street, set off firecrackers, wave a big flag . . . You know what day it's going to be, Jax? The Fourth of July. Freedom day. You bet.

JAX. One letter.

BAXTER. Are you going to die tonight, Jax? Are you?

JAX. One last letter.

BAXTER. We'll throw the blanket over your face and quietly, very quietly, unheard and unseen, we'll carry you downstairs, bed and all, and we'll dump you in the lot by the laundry with all the dog crap and rusty tin cans . . .

JAX. There'll be more room for you, more room for him.

BAXTER. All right. Fine. I agree. What's the letter?

JAX. Write in ink.

BAXTER. (*Protesting*) Do you want me to . . .

JAX. Write in ink.

BAXTER. (*Giving in*) All right. In ink. Can I bring my chair into your room, next to your bed?

JAX. No. Write.

BAXTER. (*Seated in his "room"*) Go ahead.

JAX. "To the Atomic Energy Commission. Keep up your good work. Best regards." Sign my name. Mail it.

BAXTER. Is that all?

JAX. That's all.

BAXTER. (*Rising*) And now?

JAX. (*Intoning*) Now, now, now, now . . .

BAXTER. Jax, it's not out of hate, you understand that. Sometimes, I . . . I feel very close to you and . . . I think of you a lot; an awful lot. These past few days, when I was drinking, I remember how often I used to think of you, back here in the room, and I . . . I envied you, Jax. I envied you!

JAX. When we were boys on the cracked and broken streets . . .

BAXTER. (*With a slight, almost hysterical laugh*) That's right. The three of us, always together, inseparable . . . The Three Musketeers.

JAX. How we laughed in our secret caves, darkness was light, the cold was warmth, make-believe reality, reality make-believe . . . One for all and all for one.

JAX. We walked down a thousand streets, arm-in-arm, wooden swords in our belts, steel visors in our eyes . . .

BAXTER. (*Covering his face, sobbing hoarsely*) Oh, my God, my God . . .

[26

JAX. At last. It's over. Come, now; come, now; come, now . . .

> *Pause; weakly.*

Baxter?

> BAXTER *lifts his head.*

One more letter. One more. Then . . . what? The same thing over again? No. The smell will be gone. Write this, Baxter.

> BAXTER *writes.*

"To The President of the United States." Are you writing it in ink? It has to be in ink. "To The President of the United States. Let's remember Pearl Harbor. My deepest love to the family." Sign my name. Mail it.

> *Pause.*

Baxter, I hate you.

> *Silence.* BAXTER *enters* JAX's *"room," looks down at his face, slowly covers it with the blanket, then returns to his "room" where he sits in chair, head between hands.* MAX *soon enters, wearing a worn but pressed business suit, carrying a briefcase, frayed.*

BAXTER. (*In a moment*) He's . . . gone.

MAX. When?

BAXTER. A little while ago.

> MAX *starts for* JAX's *"room." From under the blanket* JAX *speaks.*

JAX. Don't come into my room.

> MAX *laughs at* BAXTER, *viciously, goes into his own "room," removes his jacket, hangs it neatly on the back of a chair, then spreads a napkin on his desk*

27]

and takes out a container of coffee, sandwich and apple from his briefcase.

BAXTER. (*To* JAX) You phony! You lying, hypocritical phony! Here, here're your letters! Paste them together and mail them yourself!

He tears letters and throws them at him.

MAX. We had it nice and quiet for the past few days. I was hoping you wouldn't come back.

BAXTER. I don't know what happened, Max; honest. I went down for a bottle of milk, that's all I had in mind. Why would I want to lie to you? I went down. I saw nothing unusual. Nothing unusual happened. Was I singing? I think I was singing. It was beautiful out. Spring, the taste of spring . . .

MAX. But you needed to taste something else, didn't you?

BAXTER. Yes, I needed it. I thought if I didn't have a drink I would have to lay down on the sidewalk, put my cheek on the curbstone, like on a guillotine, and cry and scream and kick my legs . . . They would have had to take me away. Max . . .

Moves toward him.

MAX. Stay in your own room.

BAXTER. I did some terrible things. I must have been out of my mind.

MAX. You weren't out of your mind. Don't give yourself excuses. You were merely your own obnoxious jelly-spined self.

BAXTER. Are you going to judge me? You?

[28

MAX. Yes, me! Me! The man who pays the rent, the man who bought you those clothes, the man who fed—past tense—the man who fed that fat ugly face of yours. And if you don't like it, my friend, then you can just pick yourself up and get the hell out of here. And take that foul-smelling dunghill over there with you!

JAX. When we were boys on the cracked and broken streets . . .

BAXTER. I never thought you'd yell at me like that, Max. I judge myself. I punish myself. More than you ever could.

MAX. I am eating my dinner now. Please do not disturb me.

BAXTER. You're a heartless creepy son-of-a-bitch. You don't give a damn for anyone but yourself. At least he doesn't judge, he doesn't condemn!

MAX. I condemn you, Baxter; that I do. And I detest you to the core of your obnoxious jelly-spined self!

BAXTER. Why? Why? Will you tell me that? What did I ever do to you? I respect you, Max; I always have. It's the truth. I swear it. I remember . . . There was a couple I met, an old geezer and his wife. I told them. I said, "There's only one man I know I respect. He works all day in some stinking office; at night he sits at his desk and writes until he can't keep his eyes open, until his head is too heavy for him to keep on his shoulders." Max, all I'm asking . . .

MAX. Ask me for nothing.

BAXTER. Pity? Not even pity?

MAX. For nothing.

JAX. How we laughed in our secret caves, darkness was light, the cold was warmth, make-believe reality . . .

BAXTER. (*To* JAX) Why don't you shut up! You two, you're together. You pretend you're poles apart, but at bottom you're one and the same. You're both out to get rid of me. That's what you want, isn't it? That I should curl up and die so you can throw all my stuff out, forget that I was ever alive . . . I nearly saved you the trouble.

> *Removes knife from pocket.*

I bought this. That's what happened. It was beautiful out. Spring. The first real day of spring. I heard the kids yelling and an old man honking the horn of a yellow convertible. I saw a woman on a stoop; sitting there like a piece of sculpture that had its face washed off by the rain. Then I passed a hardware store and this knife was in the window, catching the sun and noise and the old man and the woman on its silver blade. I bought it. Then I went for a beer. How many times did I put it against my naked chest and pray for it to go in, *to go in* . . .

MAX. (*Throwing away remains of meal*) You didn't have the courage to use it.

BAXTER. Would it have been courage?

MAX. For you. Yes.

BAXTER. Max, did you want me to use it?

MAX. I think it would have been best for all concerned.

JAX. Now, now, now, now . . .

BAXTER. Maybe I will. Maybe I'll surprise you. You can't tell with someone like me.

> *Stiffly.*

Max, I'd like to go down for a drink. I need a drink. Unfortunately I have no money. If you could possibly loan me . . .

     MAX *is busy writing at desk; ignores him.*

It may very well bring about the result that everyone present seems so anxious to achieve. A dollar would be sufficient. Max, a dollar . . . We're not going to spend all evening together, are we?

MAX. (*Without looking up from desk*) She said she would drop in.

BAXTER. She?

MAX. Our friend across the alley. I ran into her downstairs. We stopped and talked. Not only have we been watching her through the window but she's been watching us as well. She's seen you crying, Baxter. You should have been more discreet. And she's seen him lying in bed, whenever she's looked across she's seen him lying in bed. At first she thought he was a bundle of old rags. But after catching a glimpse of him smelling his toes one day, she came to the conclusion that he was our invalid mother.

BAXTER. (*Excitedly*) Then she's coming! She'll be here!

MAX. I expect her in a few minutes.

BAXTER. Why didn't you tell me before? I'm not washed or dressed . . .

     In front of a mirror he wets his handkerchief with his tongue and dabs it timidly on his face; he combs his hair, then changes his shirt, socks, shoes, again picking them up from the pile of clothes on the floor; he now wears the same clothes he had on originally.

How did she look? What else did she say?

MAX. Pretty. A very pretty young lady. She's a social worker, Baxter. She thinks she can be of help.

BAXTER. Help?

MAX. That's what she said. She wanted to help us.

BAXTER. Do you think . . .

MAX. What, Baxter?

BAXTER. You said she was a "nice" girl.

MAX. I didn't. But she is, Baxter.

BAXTER. Fine. I'm glad. It doesn't matter. Anything, so long as we're not stuck up here alone. Max, should I run down for some . . . some refreshments? We have nothing . . .

MAX. You mean a bottle of, say, wine?

BAXTER. It's customary . . .

MAX. No, Baxter.

BAXTER. That's all right with me. Just let her come. Let her come.

JAX. One letter. One last letter.

BAXTER. Does he have to be here, Max? He'll scare her away.

JAX. Baxter.

BAXTER. You're not talking to me, buddy.

JAX. One letter. My last word. Then . . . Darkness. Silence. Nothing. Dust for the winds.

BAXTER. Every day he sings the same stupid song.
        To JAX.

[32

What's wrong, buddy? Can't you think of something else? You're a writer, aren't you? A man of ideas, of imagination, huh? Remember, Max? Remember his telling us the books he was going to write, the great enduring lovely books?

> *To* JAX.

Well, go ahead, buddy, go ahead and write!

JAX. He was in your room.

MAX. Who's he talking to?

BAXTER. He's raving. Don't pay him any attention.

JAX. He was in your room.

MAX. (*Rising*) Were you in my room?

BAXTER. No. What the hell would I be doing in your room?

MAX. You were. I can see it in your face.

BAXTER. You're going to listen to him? That lunatic? That stinking rotting skeleton . . .

> *Without going into* BAXTER's *"room,"* MAX *slaps* BAXTER *across the face.*

MAX. Are you mortified, Baxter? Are you offended? Has the insult penetrated to the core of your sniveling craven soul? There, there's the knife. You bought it. Now use it! Use it!

JAX. Now, now, now, now . . .

BAXTER. (*Picking up knife, in a frenzy*) Who should I use it on? On me? On you? On him? Who do you want me to use it on? Just tell me! Tell me!

> *Everyone is frozen for a moment.* BAXTER's *shoulders sag. The knife falls from his hand.*

33]

MAX. Next time you come into my room, it'll be the last time.
He works on papers at desk.

JAX. The snow came down all night. We stood by the window, watching, our noses pressed to the cold glass, our tongues hanging out, as though to catch the snow. We crawled under the blanket, this blanket, and hugged each other, tightly, tightly . . .

MAX. I'm trying to work.

JAX. In the morning we got up, we dressed, we ran out . . . Into the street, the white and silvery and pristine street . . . The snow was as high as our stomachs. We rolled in the snow. We ate the snow. We buried ourselves in the snow . . .

MAX. Tell him to be quiet. I'm working.

BAXTER. Tell him yourself.
To JAX.
I remember that morning. We built an igloo, the three of us. We worked all day, without stopping. Our gloves were frozen to our fingers.

JAX. The cold was warmth.

BAXTER. The Three Musketeers.

MAX. When it got dark we sat inside the igloo and we started a fire.

BAXTER. Do you remember that fire? Do you remember that?

MAX. It burned a hole right through the roof.

BAXTER. We were choking with the damn smoke.

MAX. And the ice . . .

[34

BAXTER. Melting down our heads . . .

MAX. Soaking our clothes . . .

BAXTER. We . . . We were turning into icicles!
>MAX *and* BAXTER *break out in laughter.*

JAX. Max.

MAX. I thought we weren't talking to one another.

JAX. One letter. Please.

MAX. I have work to do.

JAX. Soon . . . Soon it'll be too late. All my studies, my contemplations . . .

MAX. Your studies? You haven't picked up a book in ten years. And what are you contemplating over there, your navel? Your toes? The stink that rises from your rotting corpse?

JAX. One letter . . .

MAX. I have a surprise for you. Your letters are stupid, inane and worthless. Now don't bother me.
>JAX *laughs mockingly.*

MAX. You have something to say?

BAXTER. Let's cut it out. She'll be here any minute.
>JAX *laughs more loudly, more viciously.*

MAX. Shut up! Shut up!
>*He goes for him.*
You son-of-a-bitch!

BAXTER. (*Holding him back*) Max! For cryin'-out-loud! She'll be up here soon.

MAX. (*To* BAXTER) Get your hands off me! Get them off!
>*He does; to* JAX.

35]

I know what you're up to. It won't work. You'll have to do it yourself.

> *Picks up knife, slides it across the floor to* JAX's *cot.*

Here, here it is, Jax. Why don't you use it?

> *Richly sarcastic.*

Come on now. Don't tell me *you* have qualms. Not the great Jax. Not our representative from the Asylum of the Living Truth. Come now, Jax. After all . . . You don't want to die of bedsores, do you?

BAXTER. (*Forced laughter*) I bet he couldn't get out of that bed if he wanted to.

MAX. We'll probably have to bury him with the bed. Like an Egyptian pharaoh with all his earthly possessions.

JAX. Listen. Listen. The black man rises from centuries of slumber. In the night he pounds his drums. In the night he makes noise, noise, noise . . .

MAX. That's right. Noise. And you'd better get used to it because there's going to be a helluva lot more of it before you succumb to those bedsores of yours.

JAX. (*Chants mockingly*) Arise ye prisoners of starvation . . . Arise ye wretched of the earth . . .

BAXTER. (*Also mockingly*) Max is right. He's right. Things are getting better all the time.

> JAX *and* BAXTER *laugh.*

MAX. (*Desperately*) Don't confuse it. Don't throw that into it. The world isn't today or yesterday; the world is tomorrow, with decent education, with science, with understanding . . .

[36

BAXTER. Make noise. Go ahead and make noise.

JAX. He doesn't know, Baxter. He's a baby. The world is a new toy for him. He wants to play with it.

BAXTER. He's in the process of enlightenment.

JAX. His book will change the course of events.

BAXTER. His work contributes to the sanity and well-being of humanity.

JAX. Peace be with you, my child.

BAXTER. Peace be with you.

MAX. Shut up! Shut up! Both of you! I know what's burning your tails. I'm not feeding you anymore.

> *To* BAXTER.

I'm not buying you booze anymore. You're on your own and it's killing you, it's killing you!

BAXTER. But you're the one that's dying, Max. Look! Look! There are worms crawling over your face; there are worms eating at your heart. Work, Max? Write, Max? Study, Max? For what? For whom?

MAX. For me, myself! To be better than you, yes, better than the both of you! To triumph over your weak, sniveling, dissipating . . .

BAXTER. There! You said it. He said it, Jax. He wants to triumph over us, over us!

JAX. I concede.

BAXTER. I concede.

JAX. We concede.

BAXTER. We all concede. There you are, Max. You won.

37]

You're top man. Better than the best of us. Is that it? Like fun it is. Triumph over yourself, buddy; over your mean little ambitious self.

MAX. I'm not ambitious. What I do isn't for me, not only for me. It's a lie! A lie!

BAXTER. Did you hear that, Jax? Did you hear him say he's not ambitious? Then he shouldn't mind being a failure, should he?

> To MAX.

Because that's what you are, buddy. A failure. Washed up. Beaten. Finished.

MAX. No. No.

BAXTER. Open your eyes! Look at yourself! Look. A sixty-buck-a-week clerk! A writer who can't write! Meat for the analyst's couch! Ten years gone by, buddy; the worms are getting fatter. Triumph over yourself. Here. This way.

> *Quickly he dashes into* JAX's *"room," picks up knife, puts it in front of* MAX.

This way. Once and for all. Triumph over yourself, Max; over yourself!

JAX. Now, now, now, now . . .

MAX. (*Trembling*) No. I won't. No. Please. No . . .

> *There is a knock on the door.*
> *Rushing to door.*

Thank God. Thank God.

> *Opens door.*

Come in. Please come in.

> ANN *enters.*

I was afraid you weren't going to make it.

ANN. That would have been unneighborly.

MAX. I'm glad you came.

ANN. I'm glad to be here. I don't believe I've met your friends; not officially, that is.

MAX. Ann, this is Baxter.

They exchange smiles.

ANN. We've seen each other lots of times.

Turning to JAX.

And this . . .

MAX. He . . . He's sleeping. He's not feeling well. I don't think we should disturb him.

JAX. When we were boys on the cracked and broken streets . . .

ANN *turns to* MAX.

MAX. That's Jax.

ANN. (*To* JAX) I've seen you before, too, Jax. But you never turn to the window. Can I . . . do anything for you?

JAX. A letter. Write a letter.

ANN. Of course.

To MAX.

May I have some paper, please?

MAX. You don't have to bother.

BAXTER. We'll write it for him later.

JAX. Now. Now.

ANN. (*To* MAX) It's really no bother.

Taking paper from desk.

I'll bring a chair to his bed, it . . .

BAXTER. No.

MAX. You can't do that.

ANN. I can't?

MAX. We each have our own furniture, our own rooms. We make it a point . . .

BAXTER. That's one of our rules. But you can sit here. In my room.

ANN. (*Ironically*) When in Rome . . . A girl always does what she's told.

   Seated in BAXTER's *"room."*

I'm ready if you are, Jax.

JAX. In ink. Write in ink. "To the Association for the Prevention of Cruelty to Animals." Do you have it?

ANN. I have it.

JAX. Read it back.

ANN. "To the Association for the Prevention of Cruelty to Animals."

JAX. That's it. Are you writing in ink?

ANN. Blue-black permanent recording ink; it's approved by all city agencies.

JAX. Good. "To the Association for the Prevention of Cruelty to Animals. Dear Sirs: You killed my brother. Rats." Sign it. Mail it for me.

   ANN *glances from* BAXTER *to* MAX.

MAX. I told you he wasn't well.

ANN. What's wrong with him?

BAXTER. He's not in his right mind.

[40

MAX. There's nothing we can do.

ANN. I can't believe that.

JAX. (*In agony*) I'm dying. Oh, God, I'm dying, and I've done nothing, I've learned nothing, I've said nothing, nothing, nothing, nothing.

ANN. Why don't you call a doctor? Or get someone up here to look after him? That's no way to treat a human being.

MAX. He's only acting that way because you're here, Ann, because he has an audience. I suggest we ignore . . .

JAX. My God. My God. What was it for? Why? Why? Why?

BAXTER. That's enough, Jax!

MAX. Cut it out, Jax!

JAX. For this? Was it for this? No, no, it couldn't be. That couldn't be, no, no . . .

ANN. (*Running to* JAX, *on her knees at his bedside*) What is it? What's wrong?

JAX. (*More calmly*) A letter. Please. One last letter.

ANN. Why don't you rest? Try to sleep.

JAX. A letter. Then . . . I'll sleep.

ANN. Promise?

JAX. I promise.

ANN. (*Rising, going to* BAXTER's "*room*") Very well. One letter.

JAX. They have to be made to understand. They have to have their lids held open; their eyes have to be made to see. Are you writing in ink?

ANN. The same as before.

JAX. Good. Write. "To the Chairman of the International Biologists Convention, Geneva." Do you have it?

ANN. I have it.

JAX. Read it back to me.

ANN. "To the Chairman of the International Biologists Convention, Geneva."

JAX. Good. Now write. "Dear Chairman: News has just reached me that your wife is running around with a chemist. Come home at once."

ANN. You don't mean . . . This is despicable of you!

MAX. I tried to warn you.

BAXTER. You're not angry, are you?

ANN. With you? Of course not. But how can you live in the same room with him?

BAXTER. That's why we have certain rules here. But let's not talk about him.

ANN. (*Pleasantly*) That's all right with me. What shall we talk about?

BAXTER. There's only one subject that interests me.

ANN. (*Avoiding his intense stare*) What do you do, Baxter?

BAXTER. Write. I'm a writer. I've been working on a novel and if it maintains its present standard I have great hopes for it.

MAX. (*At desk, writing; mutters*) He said that ten years ago.

BAXTER. I'm talking to the lady. Don't interrupt.

[42

MAX. Why don't you tell her the truth?

BAXTER. That's my affair. Butt out.
>   *To* ANN.
It kills some people to mind their own business. If it wasn't for certain obligations, Ann, I would have walked out on them long ago.

MAX. Did you hear that, Jax?

JAX. Did you hear that, Max?

MAX. I heard that, Jax.

JAX. That makes two of us, Max.

BAXTER. You see? You see what they're like?

ANN. (*To* MAX) I expected this kind of thing from him,
>   *Moves her head toward* JAX.
but I'm really, really surprised at you. Baxter, I think I ought to go.

BAXTER. (*To* MAX *and* JAX, *shouting*) Are you going to shut up now?
>   *To* ANN, *softly.*
They'll be quiet. The last thing they want is for you to leave.

ANN. That's hard to believe. Are you three related? Are you brothers?

BAXTER. We're not brothers or cousins or friends or . . . or anything. We're just stuck together, here in this lousy room. I . . . I should have gotten something for us to drink.

ANN. I don't want anything, thank you.

BAXTER. You're a social worker, aren't you?

43]

ANN. Yes. With the Welfare Department.

BAXTER. And you live alone and for the past six months you've spent your Saturday nights reading Jane Austen.

ANN. How do you know that?

BAXTER. (*Showing her toy telescope*) My secret eye.

ANN. I must remember to keep the window shade down.

BAXTER. Don't. I like watching you. That's how I spend my Saturday nights. But why you?

ANN. I don't know. After awhile going out didn't seem like much fun.

BAXTER. You didn't go out with the right people.

ANN. I didn't meet any others.

BAXTER. Until recently?

ANN. Perhaps.

BAXTER. Can I ask you a blunt question? Now I want you to answer me truthfully, no holding back. When you first saw me, what image came to your mind? I mean . . . Did I remind you of a buffalo? Think now. And look at me closely.

> *Hunching his shoulders, burying his head, etc.; unnatural voice.*

Sometimes when I look in the mirror a buffalo stares back at me. Is that it? A buffalo?

> *He moans like a buffalo.*

ANN. (*Laughing*) No, no, really . . .

BAXTER. Hmmm. I see. Well, how about a duck? Hey, I bet that's it. A girl once told me I had the most beautiful duck-eyes she ever saw.

> *Contorting himself into shape of duck.*

[44

Look closely. Is this it? A duck?

He waddles and quacks like a duck.

ANN. Nothing like that.

BAXTER. A good sign. A very good sign. I have a theory on this, based on many years of practical experience. If you meet someone and they remind you of a particular animal, whenever you see that person in the future, you're going to think of that animal. Even if you don't want to. Spontaneously. How many times do you hear husbands say to their wives, "Shut up, you old cow." Or wives say to their husbands, "You dirty dog you." You see how it all fits in? First impressions. Listen. I once went with a girl who first time I saw her reminded me of a grasshopper. A grasshopper, of all damn things. And you know I took her to the park, the last time I saw her I took her to the park, and while we were sitting on a blanket, suddenly, without rhyme or reason, she lifted up her legs, raised her eyebrows, and hopped away, plunk! plunk! plunk! I looked for that girl for hours, until it was too dark to see, but I couldn't find her. I felt pretty bad about it. I kind of liked her. To this day whenever I see a grasshopper, I instinctively bend over and whisper, "Sheila, Sheila, is that you?"

ANN. (*Laughing*) And what do I remind you of?

BAXTER. You? Of a woman.

ANN. I'm flattered.

BAXTER. It's hard for me to believe that the window isn't between us. Can I touch your face to make sure?

Gently he touches her cheek.

The closer you are, the prettier you are. Ann . . .

45]

JAX. Ann . . .

BAXTER. (*To* JAX) Shut up!

MAX. Ann . .

BAXTER. I'm talking to her! Ann, I . . . I'm afraid of saying the wrong things. Adolescent, isn't it? Look. Why don't I go down for something? That's an idea. No, no, I insist.
> *Searches his pockets.*

I . . . That's funny. Did you see my wallet, Max?

MAX. Cut it out.

BAXTER. No, I had it. I'm sure of it. Of all the lousy luck. Look, Ann, I wonder if you could possibly loan me a few dollars. I know it isn't . . .

MAX. Baxter!

JAX. Baxter!

ANN. That's all right. I don't mind.
> *Gives him money.*

BAXTER. Thanks. I will pay you back. I insist. Don't leave now. I'll be gone only a minute.
> *Exits.*

MAX. You shouldn't have done that. He's a lush, a wino. You won't see him again tonight.

ANN. Are you serious?

MAX. I'm serious.

ANN. (*Eyes downcast*) I'm sorry you told me. He seems like . . .

MAX. He seems like. I know what he seems like. Don't trust them, Ann. Neither one of them. They have no scruples,

[46

no sense of what's right or wrong. They believe in nothing, in nobody. If you knew how much I despise them . . .

ANN. Then why do you live with them? I don't understand.

MAX. We grew up together. We saw the world with the same eyes, with the same feverish excitement running through our skinny bodies. We were all right then, at the beginning.

JAX. When we were boys on the cracked and broken streets . . .

MAX. We played ball with the sun . . .

JAX. We caught lightning from the sky . . .

MAX. Remember when we went swimming in the rain, Jax? At the P.A.L. camp?

JAX. We took off all our clothes.

MAX. We hid them behind a bush.

JAX. When we came out of the water we . . . we couldn't find them.

MAX. We looked for them for hours.

JAX. Then we found a cardboard box.

MAX. We put it over our heads and we walked . . .
> *Laughing.*

We walked all the way back to the camp with that box over our heads.
> *Silent, to* ANN.

That was a long long time ago. One day we stopped laughing and we had our hands around each other's throats. I've tried to get away from them. I moved from one place to another, from one city to another, like a gypsy, but they were always there, always with me.

47]

ANN. And there's no way for you to live together?

MAX. No more. It's too late for that. Sometimes I think that my only hope is that one of us dies, at least one of us. Even if that one is myself. I'm not being a very considerate host, am I?

ANN. I just feel that I want to help, but I don't know how. There are agencies, Max . . .

MAX. That wouldn't do any good. But you can help. Don't give up on me too quickly.

ANN. Giving up is a luxury I can't afford.

MAX. Isn't there anyone . . .

ANN. Not really.

MAX. But there was someone . . .

ANN. Yes, there was someone. I was divorced by the time I was twenty. Does that surprise you?

MAX. A little. What happened?

ANN. Everything, I suppose. We ran through a lifetime of marriage in fourteen months and eight days, with no interruptions, no pauses, no breaks. From wild sophomoric passions to utter senile boredom. It became illogical for us to remain together any longer, so we added our assets, subtracted our legal expenses, divided by two, and presto! it was done. Henceforth we were going to be worldly-wise and deliriously happy. Our apprenticeship had been served. The last I heard he was living with a maiden aunt in Poughkeepsie and . . . I'm not being a very considerate guest now, am I?

MAX. You regret leaving him?

ANN. No, not leaving him. I regret not trying to stay with him.

[48

I thought . . . Why didn't I think then? I thought the easiest thing in the world is to start over again, to walk away and begin as if nothing had ever happened. How wrong I was. It's much easier to lock the door and read Jane Austen.

MAX. We have a great deal in common.

ANN. You don't mean Jane Austen?

MAX. No. I mean the strength to be alone.

ANN. Don't you believe it, Max. There's nothing I dread more. I'll tell you a secret. One night last week I went to a dance, one of those public dances they advertise in the papers. I stood against the wall and I waited. I waited. Have you ever gone through anything like that? It's really an exercise in masochism. When someone came up to me and asked me to dance it seemed like such an unsatisfactory reward that I politely said, "No, thank you," and left.

MAX. I'm glad you did.

ANN. I was just being foolish.

MAX. Don't you believe it. Would you dance with me?

ANN. Where?

MAX. Here. Now.

ANN. But there's no music . . .

MAX. We don't need any. Please.

She rises. He holds her, about to dance.

MAX. Ann . . .

JAX. Ann . . .

MAX. Don't annoy her.

JAX. Ann . . .

MAX. Be quiet!

JAX. Ann . . .

ANN. It's all right.
>*Turning to* JAX.
What is it?

JAX. Ann, forgive me.

ANN. I didn't want us to quarrel.
>*Going to him.*
Can you tell me what the trouble is?
>*Crouches at his bedside.*

JAX. I'm dying, Ann. At last . . . At last . . .

ANN. Why do you keep saying that? There's nothing physically wrong with you.
>*Turning.*
Is there anything physically wrong with him?
>MAX *shakes his head.*
There. Now why don't you try to get up? Come, I'll help you.

JAX. I can't. My legs . . . They're paralyzed. I can't move them.

ANN. You don't want to move them.
>*Turning for help.*
Max . . .

MAX. He'll suck the last drop of blood out of you, if you let him.

JAX. Ann, Anny, my heart . . . Feel my heart.
>*She doesn't.*

The beat is getting weaker, isn't it? Tell me the truth. Isn't that the truth? Soon it'll be quiet. Soon I'll feel nothing, see nothing, know nothing . . . Oh, what a farce it's been . . . What a futile stupid mockery . . .

> *He laughs painfully.*

Ann, put your hand on my forehead. Please.

> *She does so.*

How good that feels, how good . . . Ann, go away from here. Go back to your own place. They're a pair of bad actors. Don't believe them. They're the same, the same. Ann, go away . . .

MAX. Ann, don't listen to him.

> *From outside the room* BAXTER *then shouts:* "Ann! Ann!" *He enters, flushed, disheveled, out of breath.*

BAXTER. Ann . . . I was afraid you left. I suddenly said to my-self, "What if she left? What if you won't see her again?" I ran like the devil. Ann, I . . . I'm sorry about the money. I shouldn't have taken it from you.

ANN. You can return it if you wish, Baxter.

BAXTER. I . . . I don't have it right now. But as soon as I . . .

ANN. You spent it drinking, didn't you?

BAXTER. Let me explain . . .

ANN. (*Excitedly*) You don't have to explain it to me. We barely know one another. Why me?

BAXTER. Because I want to. Because there's no one else who'd listen. Ann, I've been on a binge, on a drunk . . . for the last few days. I went downstairs, I looked up and everything

51]

was so right, so perfect, the sun, the sky, the air tasted warm and clean in my throat . . . Then I looked around, at the dirty kids, at an old man hunched over the wheel of a yellow convertible, at a woman sitting on a stoop, one hand across her lap, the other holding up her chin; her eyes . . . It was her eyes. There was so much sadness in them, so much misery . . . I wanted to throw myself down on the sidewalk and dig my fingers into the concrete . . . I was so filled with her misery that I begged for pain, for my flesh to be torn, for, yes, damn it, death itself! I . . . drank instead and when you hear some of the things I did . . .

ANN. I don't want to hear. You don't know how unfair you are. I've looked forward to meeting you for months and to tell me all this now, now . . . I don't want to hear it!

MAX. Baxter!

JAX. Baxter!

MAX. Shut up!

JAX. Shut up!

BAXTER. (*Oblivious of them*) I met this couple in a bar on Third Avenue. Mr. and Mrs. Collins. They bought me a few drinks and then we went up to their place, a smelly little room near the river. They had a bottle and we drank some more. We were having quite a time for ourselves. The old man sang, he did a crazy jig and then he passed out. His wife, that's what they said she was, a fat gray-haired woman with dirty fingernails and red swollen hands . . . She crawled across the floor toward me like some mad

[52

old witch, her mouth grinning from ear to ear and . . . I
knew what I was doing. I knew it . . .

  A pause.

ANN. (*Throwing up her hands, attempts to be casual*) So
that's it. Thank you for asking me up, Max.

MAX. Are you blaming me for what he did?

ANN. I'm just very tired and I have to get up early.

MAX. A little while longer, please. Sit here, in my room. We
don't have to have anything to do with them. So far as
we're concerned they're not even here; they don't exist.

ANN. I must have had illusions of grandeur to think I could
be of help. I am sorry for them.

MAX. Don't be. That's their one consolation and they don't
deserve it. I don't want to talk about them. Ann, if you're
not busy Saturday . . . I'd like to . . .

ANN. I would too.

MAX. You know what we'll do? We'll take the 125th Street
ferry to Playland. We'll ride all the rides, eat hot dogs, drink
beer, dance out in the open . . . But we have to try everything. No excuses, no holding back . . .

ANN. Do you know, I've never been there before.

MAX. Never?

ANN. Never.

MAX. Wonderful. You don't know what you've missed. It's
. . . Come to think of it I've never been there myself.

  ANN *laughs.*

It's good to hear you laugh.

ANN. Can't you laugh?

MAX. I'm going to let you teach me. Ann . .

> *He takes her hands; reluctantly she pulls them away.*

ANN. We have to talk.

MAX. (*Takes her hands again*) I don't feel like talking.

ANN. I want to know more about you.

MAX. I want to know nothing.

ANN. You haven't even told me what you do.

MAX. Write. I'm a writer. I've been working on a novel . . .

BAXTER. (*Muttering*) He said that ten years ago.

JAX. Don't believe him, Ann.

MAX. Ignore them. Don't pay any attention to them.

BAXTER. Ask him to show you what he wrote tonight.

MAX. (*To* BAXTER) You open your mouth again . . .

JAX. Ask him for the truth, the truth.

ANN. May I see what you wrote, Max?

MAX. Nothing. I haven't been writing lately. Just notes, ideas . . . There's nothing I can show you.

BAXTER. On his desk. Look on his desk.

ANN. (*Picks up paper from desk*) It's a letter. Is this what you wrote?

> *No answer; reading.*

"To the Honorable Russian Delegate to the United Nations, New York City. Dear Sir: Six o'clock. Tuesday morn-

ing. Bring woolen socks and a bottle of ginger ale."
> *Drops letter.*

I don't understand.

MAX. It's nothing. I wrote it for Jax. It's his letter. Jax, tell her! Tell her!

JAX. When we were boys on the cracked and broken streets . . .

MAX. Ann, listen to me.

JAX. Ann, forgive me.

BAXTER. Ann, let me explain.

ANN. (*Turning, restrained hysteria*) What is it you want from me? Will you please let me know what you want from me?
> *Pause.*

BAXTER. (*Softly*) Nothing. Nothing at all. I hope you have better luck next time.
> ANN *slumps onto a footstool; she doesn't cry but wipes her eyes with a handkerchief.*

I did those things deliberately, Ann. I wanted to become so ashamed of myself, so disgusted with what I was that the rest would have been easy.

JAX. He bought a knife.

MAX. He was going to kill himself.

ANN. (*Looking up at* BAXTER) No. You weren't . . .

BAXTER. (*Taking knife from desk, pressing it into palm of hand*) I couldn't. We don't know how much we love our own rotting flesh until it's cut, until the blood spurts out . . .

ANN. Stop that!
> *Takes knife from him.*
Now look what you've done. Does that give you pleasure?

BAXTER. Your anxiety gives me pleasure.

ANN. Let me bandage it.
> *Does so with handkerchief.*

JAX. We went to the park, on a Sunday morning, the three of us. We took our guns, our swords, and filled our knapsack with apples and a canteen of water.

MAX. How we laughed in our secret caves, darkness was light, the cold was warmth, make-believe reality . . .

BAXTER. We buried our knapsack under a large stone and then we ran and shouted . . .

JAX. Conquering new worlds, proclaiming ourselves to be masters . . .

MAX. Over the rocks, around the edge of the lake, and up the tallest tree . . .

BAXTER. Where we sang out at the top of our lungs, "I am the king of the universe . . ."

JAX. And raised our fist to the sky.

MAX. And raised our fist to the sky.

ANN. There. It should be all right now.

MAX. Do you have to go, Ann?

ANN. You give me no choice.

MAX. Will I see you Saturday?

[56

ANN. I don't think so. I am sorry. Good night.
> *Looks at others.*

Good night.
> *Quickly exits.*
>
> MAX *and* BAXTER *slump into chairs in their respective "rooms." There is a moment of heavy silence.*

BAXTER. We shouldn't have let her go.

MAX. What do you suggest? That we tied her up and locked her in the closet?

BAXTER. That's right. Anything. Anything but this . . . I didn't get a chance to talk to her, to explain . . .

MAX. You talked too damn much.

BAXTER. I'm not asking you. Don't you understand that?

MAX. You talked too damn much.

JAX. You talked too damn much.

MAX. You talked too damn much.

JAX. You talked too damn much.

MAX. You talked too damn much.

JAX. You talked too damn much.

BAXTER. (*Rises, fists clenched impotently*) Shut up! Shut up!
> *He glares at both of them, then slowly, wearily, sits down.*

JAX. (*Shortly*) She was very pretty. And intelligent. You could see it in her eyes; in her sense of humor. I could smell the scent of her body. It's just as well she left. I'm glad. Write a letter for me, Max.

57]

MAX. (*Shaking his head in anguish*) You won't die. You won't die.

BAXTER. I need a drink. God . . . Oh, God . . .

JAX. Soon it'll be over. Soon . . . Soon . . .

MAX. I'm going to work.
> At desk, moves papers about.

I have my work to do.

BAXTER. You should have touched her hair and her eyes and her lips . . .

JAX. Now, now, now, now . . .

MAX. I'll finish it. Whatever you say . . . Whatever you try to do . . . I'll finish it and it'll be there; it'll be done. Something I did.

BAXTER. (*Rising; cries in pain*) Max!

MAX. Go away. Let me work.

BAXTER. Max!

MAX. I have to work, I said!

BAXTER. (*Almost with a sob*) A drink, Max. I need a drink!

MAX. (*Rises and rushes toward* BAXTER) I'll kill you! I swear I'll kill you!
> *The two men grab each other around the throat, struggle back and forth, sobbing and panting loudly. The lights dim and only their shadows loom largely on the wall behind them.*

JAX. (*Slowly*) When we were boys on the cracked and broken

[58

streets . . . We laughed in our secret caves . . . Darkness was light, the cold was warmth . . . Make-believe reality . . . Reality make-believe . . .

LIGHTS OUT

CURTAIN

WINDOWS

WINDOWS

SCENE:

The living room on the ground floor of a one-family house in Blakeville, a small community outside of the City. Littered about are boxes, debris, planks of wood, a ladder, etc. The only furniture is a number of mismatched wooden chairs and a folded gateleg table, all too worthless to have been taken. The entrance door and a window are in the left wall; three unusually large windows are in the rear wall, a door to the kitchen and a staircase leading to the second floor are in the right wall.

The stage is in darkness. The front door opens. A faint beam of light falls on the floor. TED *and* FRANCES ATKINS (*a tall sallow-skinned couple in their forties, eyes bleary from lack of proper sleep —*FRANCES *is eight months pregnant) enter with packages and suitcases.*

TED. Watch yourself.

FRANCES. It has a funny smell.

TED. It's the oldest house around here; that's why I took it. But it's comfortable: seven rooms and the garden out front . . .

FRANCES. The lights, Ted. Where are the . . .

TED. I'm looking for them. They should be somewhere along . . .

> FRANCES *turns on the light.* TED *rises from the floorboard where his hand has wandered in search of the light switch.* FRANCES *looks about; she spots the windows at once; there is anguish in her voice.*

FRANCES. Ted, there are windows; there are windows!

TED. Of course there are windows. You didn't think . . .

FRANCES. (*Hurriedly pulling the faded musty drapes over all the windows*) You know, you know, and yet . . . It's the same thing. Over and over again.

TED. What did you want me to do? Do you think I could find something to our particular specifications?

FRANCES. The windows didn't have to be that large, that many. And the lights I saw outside. We're stuck right in the middle of all those houses, aren't we? Right in the middle!

TED. That's how they build nowadays. Damn them. What do you want from me? I had to take what I could get. And this was the best, for the money . . .

> *Going to her.*

Fran. There won't be any trouble. No trouble.

> *Points to windows.*

Do you see the way they are now? That's the way they're going to be, so long as we live here. If you want, get new drapes, a brighter color, and when I'm at the school, you can change them and . . . That's the way they'll be, undisturbed, untouched. You have my word, my solemn word . . .

FRANCES. I know. We've had this conversation before, too.

[64

TED. (*Bitter laugh*) That's right. Let's quarrel. Our first night here. What else could we do?

FRANCES. We could leave. Right now. We could take our things and shut that door . . .

TED. And what? Go where? I paid a year's rent on this place. I have to be at work Monday morning . . .
>*Shouting.*

Will you stop creating more problems for us than is necessary! That's what you do. You create . . .
>*She turns away from him; softer tone.*

Fran, it'll be all right. It won't be like last time.

FRANCES. (*Wearily*) And the time before that.

TED. And the time before that.

FRANCES. And the time before that.

TED. And . . . Do you want to leave? Do you?
>*No answer.*

If you want to leave, we'll leave, and that's all there is to it.

FRANCES. Do you want to leave?

TED. Don't ask me. I'm asking you.

FRANCES. I can ask your opinion, can't I?

TED. Why should we leave? It's not a bad place. You have to look at the rooms upstairs. They left a bed, an old brass bed; it's really an antique. And the garden. Sunday mornings we could plant things, potter about . . .

FRANCES. I couldn't see it in the dark. Is it . . . open?

TED. There's a fence on both sides; a thick wooden fence. We'll have all the privacy we want. Fran. The school I'll

65]

be working at. I've got a good program. Two bright classes and I can even get home for lunch during the day. It's only five minutes from here.

FRANCES. If you told me about the windows before I came . . .

TED. (*Getting angry*) Let's not kid each other, for God's sake. You didn't come with me because you knew I'd have to take a place like this. But you wanted to be free of that decision. Was it because you could enjoy being critical now? Is that it?

FRANCES. It's not true. You know it's not.

TED. Then let's stop it. The other times . . . The windows . . . Was it all my fault? All of it? Each and every time?
>*She doesn't answer.*

It's in the past, hon. We can forget it now. We both learned our lesson. Look. Look at this room. Isn't it tremendous?

FRANCES. We won't have enough furniture.

TED. We'll buy more. I noticed a couple of antique shops on one of the side streets. I bet we could pick up some things at a damn reasonable price.
>*They start unpacking some of the boxes—FRANCES has put one on the table, removes dishware, odds-and-ends, etc.*

FRANCES. Don't ask anyone to visit us. Not even from the school.

TED. Not till you say so.

FRANCES. Well, I'm not going to say so for a very long time.

[66

It'll take us months to get this place looking right. And then it'll take me a very long time to get over . . .

She touches her stomach.

TED. There's no hurry. How silly you are.

FRANCES. I'll have to drop in at the hospital . . .

TED. They have all your records. I checked on that.

FRANCES. I couldn't help noticing. There's a house a few feet from that window . . .

Points to window in rear, left.

TED. Why do you have to go into it? Who cares?

FRANCES. Is there anything wrong in speaking about it? That's part of the trouble, you know. I don't have the least reluctance . . .

TED. All right, all right. Speak about it. Go ahead. Speak about it.

FRANCES. All I wanted to say is that there's a house a few feet from that window . . .

Points to window again.

And another house behind that window.

Points to window in rear, right.

TED. (*Indifferently*) Good.

FRANCES. Can you see any other houses from the kitchen?

TED. (*Mockingly*) Yes, you can see a house, a single house, from the kitchen. And from the rooms upstairs you can see exactly five houses, all neatly crowded together, including the two houses you previously referred to: one behind that window

Points.

and one behind the other window.
> *Points.*

Is my report satisfactory?

FRANCES. There's nothing to be afraid of.

TED. Good.

FRANCES. Nor any reason why we can't talk.

TED. Good. Now that you've cleared all that up, will you do me a favor and look at the kitchen? You haven't seen the place and already you're worried about what's going on outside.
> *He leads her to the kitchen. She goes inside. He remains on the threshold.*

FRANCES. I have time. I know it's got everything.

TED. (*Stares at windows, kneading his hands*) What do you think?
> *He moves toward windows, then turns back decisively.*

FRANCES. (*Offstage; appropriate sounds*) Plenty of closet space. We'll have to take the top off this range and soak it in hot water. New linoleum.
> *Comes out.*

Nice. I never had a kitchen that big before.

TED. And upstairs, four rooms, four of them. The bedroom has the beams exposed, running right across the ceiling.

FRANCES. (*Unpacking*) We really didn't need this many rooms. Oh, I know you couldn't get anything smaller. And we did get a bargain, considering what you paid.

[68

TED. Why don't we call your brother? He said he'd like to see the house.

FRANCES. We haven't been here ten minutes and you have to have someone . . .

TED. It was just an idea. He's your brother. If you don't want to call him, we won't call him. It doesn't make any difference to me.

FRANCES. We don't need anyone tonight.
>   *Slight pause.*
How do you feel?

TED. I feel fine. You?

FRANCES. My headache's almost gone. You'll be able to work here, Ted. It seems nice and quiet.
>   *He nods.*
I want you to work, start writing again. You'll have the time and there's no reason why you shouldn't go back to it now.

TED. We'll see.

FRANCES. You should. And you don't have to teach full-time anymore.

TED. Do we go through this again?

FRANCES. But I don't want you doing something you don't want to do. You don't have to now.

TED. I want to. Plain and simple. I want to. I find nothing objectionable in teaching full-time. On the contrary, I enjoy it. I enjoy paying the bills myself and going off to work in the morning and . . . All right, so I started so you could have the baby but even . . .

69]

> FRANCES' *face takes on a pained expression; she sits in a chair, holds her stomach.*
> *Feelingly.*

Fran.

FRANCES. What do I do? What *do* I do?

TED. (*On his knee by her chair*) Wait. Another two weeks at the most and then it'll be gone.

FRANCES. It will be gone and that'll be the end of that.

TED. We managed before.

FRANCES. We did. We managed. We were even happy, weren't we? We were happy!

TED. We had each other. You can't forget that. And we have each other now.

FRANCES. That's true. I believe that. The others . . .

> *Rising, shouting at windows.*

They can die! They can die like this thing inside me!

TED. (*Rising*) To hell with them. All of them. We don't need them. We never did need them.

FRANCES. Die! Die! All of you!

TED. (*Also shouting at windows*) Stuck-up illiterate louses!

FRANCES. Snobs! Hypocrites!

TED. Foul-mouthed sniveling imbeciles!

FRANCES. (*Laughing almost hysterically*) Good for you.

> *At windows.*

Foul-mouthed sniveling imbeciles!

TED. (*Laughing with same note of hysteria*) Low-brow lecherous lumpheads!

[70

FRANCES. Wonderful!
> *At windows.*

Low-brow lecherous lumpheads!

TED. Listen to this one. Listen.
> *At windows.*

Ill-conceived cretinous . . .

FRANCES. (*Suddenly turns to him; shrieks*) Ted!

TED. (*He holds her tightly*) You're all right. You're going to be fine.

FRANCES. It's dead. And I can't get it out. I can't.

TED. Soon. Soon, honey.

FRANCES. It's in my stomach and in my head and in my mouth . . .

TED. Soon. It'll be gone.
> *Gently touches her face.*

My wife.

FRANCES. Yes.

TED. In all the years I never wanted or needed . . .

FRANCES. We were happy, weren't we?

TED. At times, very very happy.

FRANCES. And lonely. Hours and hours . . .

TED. (*Moving away*) Bad luck or . . . something. We know people, usually, but . . . Somehow we always seem to be alone.

FRANCES. (*Sits in chair*) The baby . . . We needed the baby, Ted. We wanted the baby. Don't pretend now. Please.

71]

He doesn't answer her; dully.
We won't have another chance.

TED. (*Stays with original thought*) Fran, listen. We are what we are. We're not going to change at this date.

FRANCES. I didn't care one way or the other until the doctor said, "I'm sorry. I am sorry."

TED. Why should we change? I don't know how to flirt with other women and you don't know how to gossip all afternoon. That's our strength, not our weakness.

FRANCES. (*Rises, unpacks*) We never stayed in one place long enough to meet the right people.

TED. Three years in Lynwood. That should have been long enough. No, that isn't it. I'm just asocial or . . .

FRANCES. You are not and don't say it.

TED. I didn't. Fred . . . What was his name? In Lynwood. Fred Wirtz. He said it.

FRANCES. Fred Wirtz. A lot he knows. He said that because you showed him what a lumphead he was. Trying to talk about literature . . .

TED. I can't play it their way. Either you know what you're talking about or you shut up. Talk for the sake of talking . . .

FRANCES. I'm the one who can't get along with people. Not you. I alienate them. I know I do.

TED. You do not. And I forbid you . . .

FRANCES. I don't care. I can't pretend I feel affection for someone when I don't.

[72

TED. Aw, the hell with them. I've got it. Why don't we call your brother? He can . . .

> *She turns to him; he gives it up.*

All right. Forget it. Maybe Sunday.

FRANCES. (*Dully*) Maybe.

TED. It's not important.

FRANCES. (*Dully*) No.

TED. We managed . . .

FRANCES. (*Dully*) Yes.

TED. (*Shouting*) Will you stop now? Will you stop it!

FRANCES. (*Also shouting*) Stop what? What am I doing?

TED. You know damn well what you're doing!

FRANCES. I don't know. If I knew I wouldn't ask you!

TED. You're doing nothing. Nothing at all. It's all my imagination. You always sound like that.

FRANCES. I wasn't . . .

> *Gives it up, tries to sound interested.*

We can use the bed upstairs tonight, can't we?

TED. (*Nods*) I'll get the sheets.

> *Removes them from package.*

FRANCES. We'll have to call a man in to scrape the floor.

TED. I thought I'd do it myself. Rent one of those machines and save a few dollars.

FRANCES. I hope the furniture comes early.

TED. They said before noon.

FRANCES. There's so much to do. We'll be busy for weeks.

TED. We *will* be busy.

FRANCES. I'll take those.

> *Takes sheets from him.*

Be right down.

TED. (*Softly urgent*) Fran.

> FRANCES *moves ahead without turning or acknowledging he spoke to her. She climbs stairs and exits.* TED *drops his hands to his sides; he walks about, feeling ill, depressed. He hits the drapes, contemptuously; he can't move away from them. He wipes his brow, his hands; then turns impetuously and sticks his head between the folds of the drapes, at the window, rear, left. The sound of* FRANCES *returning causes him to move back and assume an air of innocence.*

FRANCES. (*Almost brightly*) I forgot a pillowcase. The rooms are large. And why didn't you tell me about the paneling? It's beautiful.

> *Searches for pillowcase.*

TED. (*Overzealous*) Did you see the small room up front?

FRANCES. Where the roof slants?

TED. That's it. You know whose room that's going to be, don't you?

FRANCES. Your shelves won't fit on those walls.

TED. Built-in shelves would. I can cut down the shelves I have now and . . .

> *The telephone rings. It is on the floor in the rear, obscured.* FRANCES *looks around for it.* TED *stands still, kneading his hands.*

[74

FRANCES. Where's that coming from? It . . .

> *Stands over phone.*

You didn't give this number to anyone, did you, Ted?

TED. I don't even know what the number is. Let it ring. It's probably for the people who moved out.

FRANCES. You can't let it ring and . . .

> *Looks at windows; soberly.*

Answer it, Ted.

TED. Why do I have to answer it? What're you building? You always create situations . . .

FRANCES. (*Loudly*) Will you *please* answer it?

> TED *stares at her a moment, then picks up phone.*

TED. Hello. I'm afraid you have the wrong number. No, no, you . . . Who? Mr. Pearce? Yes, Mr. Pearce. Well, to tell you the truth we only just got in and . . . I wasn't . . . No, I was not. I . . .

> *Angrily.*

All right. Don't make a federal case out of it. I understand thoroughly!

> *He slaps receiver into cradle, turns to* FRANCES *who is now seated in chair.*

I just . . .

FRANCES. (*Dully*) I know. You just wanted to see what they were doing.

TED. No. Not even that. I . . .

FRANCES. I know.

TED. If they didn't build these damn houses so close together . . .

FRANCES. It doesn't make sense. You have willpower, you do, and for something like this . . .

TED. Look, hon . . . I'll go over there and I'll . . . I'll apologize to them. I won't have this hanging over our heads. I'll settle it and it'll be over. Do you agree? Don't you think that's best?

> FRANCES *nods without conviction.*

All right. I'll be back in a minute. I know just what to say.

> TED *exits.* FRANCES *takes some pins from a box, goes to window, rear, right, and starts pinning drapes together, from shoulder level down to the floor. Gradually her determination to seal the drapes gives way to curiosity—she shakes her head, pulls down on her cheeks, shows irritation with herself and her own impulses; and when she is on her knees, pinning drapes—she bangs the floor with her fists in frustration; she looks about, ferret-like, then crawls under the drapes and disappears on the other side of them, completely hidden from view but standing, her outline visible.* TED *enters.*

TED. Fran! Fran! Fran!

> *Not seeing her he rushes upstairs. The outline of* FRANCES *moves behind the drapes to the left side of the room. As soon as* TED *exits she comes out from behind the drapes, first straightens her clothes, her hair, then shouts.*

FRANCES. Ted! Ted!

TED. (*Coming down*) Where were you? I saw him, Fran.

[76

Mr. Pearce. I explained just what happened and we shook hands; there'll be no trouble now.

FRANCES. Let's finish unpacking.

TED. How's your headache?

FRANCES. The same. You're all right, aren't you?

TED. Fine.

FRANCES. Your shoulder?

TED. Haven't felt anything in days. They were having a party over there. Twisting and whatnot. It's what I said before: you can't get in with these people unless you're willing to assume certain characteristics.

FRANCES. I can do without it.

TED. (*Softly*) Fran.
> *She turns to him; he holds her.*

FRANCES. I didn't mean to sound like a shrike.

TED. You don't think I'm a bad guy?

FRANCES. Not if you kiss me.
> *He kisses her. The phone in the kitchen rings.* TED *moves slowly away from* FRANCES, *the expression on his face hardens.*
> *Defensively.*
It's not our phone. It's not.

TED. In the kitchen. There's a phone in the kitchen.

FRANCES. Why would they have two phones?

TED. How do I know why they would have two phones. Just go in and answer it.

77]

FRANCES. (*Moving toward kitchen*) It couldn't be for us.

TED. Answer it! And don't keep saying I'm the only one. That's what gets me so damn angry!

FRANCES.
> *Stands on kitchen threshold with phone.*

Hello. Yes, Mrs. who? Mrs. Ryan. Yes, Mrs. Ryan. I . . . I am sorry if you felt that I was looking . . . I did look out but my thoughts were elsewhere and I can assure you . . .

TED. (*Talks as* FRANCES *talks on phone, moves about*) I'm glad this happened tonight. I am sincerely glad. It proves once and for all that I'm not the only one.

FRANCES. (*Into phone*) Believe me, I want my privacy as much as you want yours, Mrs. Ryan.

TED. Apologize to her. Don't beat around the bush. That's your . . .
> *The living-room phone rings.* TED *looks down at it, dumbly.*

FRANCES. (*Holding hand over mouthpiece; shouting*) Upstairs! You looked out the window upstairs, didn't you?
> *Into phone.*

Yes, Mrs. Ryan. I can assure you . . .
> *To* TED; *shouting.*

Answer it! Answer it!
> FRANCES *enters kitchen to continue her conversation.* TED *picks up phone.*

TED. Mr. Atkins here. Yes, Mrs. . . . Haines. Well, it's this way, Mrs. Haines: our upstairs window is very close to your upstairs window and we just came in a little while ago; I

[78

was really checking the windows . . . I wasn't staring. I couldn't care less . . . Yes. Yes. But I did not deliberately . . .

> *As* TED *talks he inadvertently pulls the drape aside and looks out; realizing at once what he has done, he drops the drape and slaps his hand to his forehead; his face loses its color. Emptily.*

It . . . It won't happen again. Yes, I understand. I . . .

> FRANCES *enters, moves toward a chair. The kitchen phone rings again. Without hesitating she makes an about-face, moves back to the kitchen, slowly, lifelessly.*

FRANCES. We have to get curtains . . . for the kitchen window.

TED. (*Nods sadly; then into phone*) Right. I agree, Mrs. Haines. I do. Right.

> *He puts receiver into cradle, holds phone, waiting.*

FRANCES. (*Offstage, answering phone*) Yes. Yes. We haven't had time, frankly . . . There will be curtains . . . Yes. Yes.

> *The living-room phone rings.* TED *lifts receiver.*

TED. Mr. Pearce? Hi, there. I know. Yes. I . . .

> *He holds phone away from his ear a moment.*

My sincerest . . . My apologies, Mr. Pearce.

> *Hangs up; puts phone back on floor.*
> FRANCES *enters. They both sit down in chairs, forlornly. A long pause.* FRANCES *rises, unpacks.*

TED. They don't give you a chance.

79]

FRANCES. We ask for trouble.

TED. I hate myself. At times like this I really hate myself.

FRANCES. It's a pattern we developed. We can't break it.

TED. We can't.

FRANCES. You ought to take the suitcases upstairs.

TED. I will. Fran?

He waits until she turns to him.

I intend to start writing again. I'm only at the school until three; that still leaves me plenty of time.

FRANCES. It will make me feel a lot better. You should never have stopped.

TED. Then it's settled.

FRANCES. Why don't you send the things you wrote off to that agent . . .

TED. I will. Definitely.

FRANCES. It used to be so important to you. You wouldn't think of doing anything else. Only enough for bread. That's what you used to say. And I was very proud of myself for seeing to it that you weren't hampered by extra expenses or extra responsibilities. I wanted you to write, to do what you wanted. Nothing else mattered to me. Not even having children.

TED. We grew up, that's all.

FRANCES. But once we decided to have the baby, once I felt that you meant it . . .

TED. If you had said anything at any time . . .

FRANCES. I know. For me, you would have done it. You would

[80

have. I know. But I didn't want it that way. And my good common sense saw nothing so very wrong in not having children. Ever. People with money can afford children, we said. The rich life is the free life, we said. We had each other. But once we changed our minds, it became more and more important . . . To give birth. Why was that suddenly so important to us?

TED. (*Almost in anger*) I don't know.

FRANCES. Nothing more important. To give birth. To do this one thing that went deeper than my good common sense. And I couldn't. I couldn't, Ted. I tried, for both of us; I tried, I did . . .

TED. (*Shouting in pain*) Enough! That's enough!
> *He embraces her, not out of desire but out of anguish, kisses her neck, her cheeks, her brow, frantically.*
Fran. Fran. My wife. Fran. Fran.

FRANCES. (*Not sobbing but tears flooding her eyes, holding him away*) Let me kiss you. Once. Please. Please.
> *She kisses him on the lips.* TED *breaks away, speaks excitedly, urgently.*

TED. We have work to do. Plenty of work to do. We can fix this place so that it's really something.

FRANCES. There will be plenty to do.

TED. Renovate the whole house, from top to bottom.

FRANCES. I'm anxious to see those antique stores. I'd love to get an old butcher's table.

TED. In a town like this, you can still find them.

81]

FRANCES. And you know what I was thinking, Ted. If we wall-papered this room instead of painting it, with that striped paper we saw . . .

TED. It's an idea.

FRANCES. It would cost more.

TED. That's all right. What colors would you use?

FRANCES. We'd have to take them out of the rug, probably blue and . . .

> *With sudden indignation.*

They were nasty and rude. I don't care what we did, it doesn't excuse their being nasty and rude.

TED. They couldn't wait. Did you notice that? It didn't take them thirty seconds to get on the phone . . .

FRANCES. And not one of them had the decency to ask if there was an explanation . . .

TED. Or extenuating circumstances. There could have been.

FRANCES. At least they could have asked. But they weren't interested in making us feel welcome; that was the least thing they had in mind.

TED. What gets me is why we're always so damn defensive! Rudeness has to be answered with rudeness.

FRANCES. Is there a phone book around?

TED. (*Looking about for one*) There should be. What are you thinking?

FRANCES. I'd like to give them some of their own medicine. The nerve of some people; it's incredible.

> TED *has found the phone book.*

Let me . . .

[82

TED. Wait. I know how to handle this.

> *Looks through book.*

Mr. Pearce. Mr. . . . Pearce. Here it is. He'll be number one.

> *Dials.*

Shhh, now. Don't make any noise.

> TED *waits until the ring is answered, then he laughs into mouthpiece—a sinister ghoulish cackle out of a horror film.* FRANCES *clenches her teeth to keep from laughing aloud.* TED *puts the phone to* FRANCES' *ear so that she can hear Mr. Pearce's frustrated protests.* TED *cackles into the mouthpiece once more, puts down receiver; they both break into laughter.*

There. That . . . That'll show them.

FRANCES. It's too much.

TED. I wish I could . . . have seen him.

FRANCES. Oh, no. That would . . . That would knock me out completely. Now I go. It's my turn now, Ted. Can you find Mrs. Ryan's number? Is she in there?

TED. (*Finding number, then dialing for her*) Mrs. Ryan it is.

FRANCES. Why didn't we ever do this before?

TED. Fools. We were fools.

FRANCES. Cowards. That's what we were.

TED. (*Whispering as he hands her phone*) Mrs. Atkins. Mrs. Ryan.

> FRANCES *hoots like an owl.* TED *adds his voice to hers, cackling like a witch.* TED *tries to get the phone away from her but she holds it out of his*

83]

> *reach. It takes all their willpower to keep from laughing aloud. The doorbell rings. Their faces change to expression of utter dismay.* FRANCES *puts down the phone.*

FRANCES. (*Apprehensively*) Is that the front door?

TED. (*Nods*) We're in for trouble now.

FRANCES. How did they know?

TED. Beats me.

FRANCES. How stupid, childish of us.

TED. I have to answer it.

FRANCES. Yes.

TED. God damn it.

> *He goes to door, shaking his head. He opens the door and three figures enter, all masked:* LESTER HAINES, *a tall dark-haired boy, nineteen, in sweat-shirt;* KAREN COLLINS, *a slim pretty girl, seventeen, in rolled-up jeans; and* EUGENE OLOFF, *a short chubby boy, also nineteen. The masks they wear are the grotesque rubber "monster" masks sold in cheap souvenir shops.*

LESTER. Trick or treat?

TED. Who are . . .

KAREN. Trick or treat?

EUGENE. Trick or treat?

TED. (*To Frances*) It isn't Halloween, is it?

LESTER. (*Removes mask*) Nah. It's April Fool's, not Halloween.

[84

Laughing.

Nah. It's not even April Fool's. That passed. We came over to welcome you. We heard you first moved into the neighborhood and we're like a welcoming committee; yeah, a self-appointed welcoming committee.

TED. That is thoughtful . . .

      KAREN *and* EUGENE *sing in unison.*

KAREN *and* EUGENE.
We welcome you,
We welcome you,
We're glad to extend
Our hand to you.
We welcome you.
We welcome you,
So long as you're not
A Nigger or a dirty Jew.
      They laugh, remove masks.

FRANCES. (*Shrugging; involuntary laugh*) At least they're honest.

TED. Honest, yes; but what does it mean?

LESTER. It means we're glad to have you in the neighborhood, Mr. Atkins.

TED. You know me?

LESTER. Sure. We've been waiting to meet you all week.

TED. You're not students at the high school, are you?

LESTER. Sure. Well, sort of. We're skipping this term. But we'll be back next term.

KAREN. I'm Karen Collins.

85]

EUGENE. Eugene Oloff.

LESTER. Lester Haines, Mr. Atkins.
Shakes his hand.

TED. Mrs. Atkins . . .

LESTER. (*Shakes her hand*) Glad to meet you, Mrs. Atkins.

TED. (*To Karen*) Too bad you're not going to school this term. That song you just sang . . .

KAREN. A lot of that goes on around here.

EUGENE. Plenty of it. We could tell you . . .

KAREN. Everybody says one thing but means something else.

LESTER. Like our politicians.

EUGENE. Yeah, like our politicians. They talk about peace but what they want all the time is war.

LESTER. We're tired of all that yak-yak. You see, Mr. Atkins, we kids today, we don't accept double-talk. I mean, we want more than words; we want action.

EUGENE. What did we get for being in two wars? My brother was killed in the war!

LESTER. You don't have a brother, will you shut up? You see, Mr. Atkins, the younger generation of kids today have both their feet on the ground. They're not taken in by fancy speeches and a lot of talk like kids from other generations.

TED. That's all to the good, I agree. But still . . .

KAREN. And what about the grown-ups, the so-called guardians of our society? All they do is keep things in the dark. They don't have the courage to do them out in the open. Right, Les?

[86

LESTER. Right.

EUGENE. (*To Lester*) Let me have the keys, huh?

LESTER. Hold your horses.

KAREN. Like the people who used to live here, for one example.

TED. Wallace?

KAREN. Wallace.
> *Wags her hand.*
Boy, what went on . . .

FRANCES. (*Curiously*) What went on?

LESTER. It's not nice to talk about, Mr. Atkins.

KAREN. We wouldn't talk about it.

EUGENE. My sister could tell you plenty.

LESTER. You don't have a sister. Will you shut up?

TED. You must be exaggerating. I only met them once but I saw nothing . . .

LESTER. (*To Karen*) Ha, did you hear that?

KAREN. (*Laughing*) He saw nothing.

EUGENE. (*To Lester; laughing*) He wasn't looking in the right place.

KAREN. (*Wags her hand*) Boy . . .

LESTER. We better change the subject.

KAREN. Yeah, let's talk about something else.

FRANCES. Oh, no. Ohhh, no. Not now you don't!

TED. (*Reprimandingly*) Fran.

FRANCES. They might as well finish. You know it isn't polite to start something and not finish.

>*To Lester.*

What about them?

LESTER. Okay. If you want us to finish. But we're going to have to spell it out for you. O.

KAREN. R.

EUGENE. G.

LESTER. I.

KAREN. E. S.

FRANCES. Here? In this . . .

>*They nod solemnly.*

TED. No. I don't believe it. This is not right. It's not.

LESTER. Okay. Okay, Mr. Atkins. You don't have to believe us. But it's a fact.

KAREN. That's what you get when you try to tell the truth.

>*They start to leave.*

EUGENE. It's the same thing when I talk to my father.

>*To Lester; vehemently.*

You going to say I don't have a father, huh? You going to say it?

LESTER. (*Shrugging him off*) What a character.

FRANCES. (*Anxiously*) You're not leaving? Don't. Please. You don't have to leave now. It's early and we weren't planning to do anything that can't wait. Ted . . .

TED. (*Also anxiously*) You don't want us to be accused of being inhospitable, do you? Give us a chance. We have no

[88

entertainment for you but . . . Fran, isn't there something we can serve . .

FRANCES. Wine. Why didn't I think of it? I could make a punch. How does that sound?
> *They return to their seats.*

EUGENE. Sounds great to me.

LESTER. You don't have to bother mixing the wine, Mrs. Atkins.

FRANCES. It'll taste better.
> *Lifts box, moves to kitchen.*
Would you like to help, Karen?

KAREN. Not particularly.

FRANCES. (*To Ted, smiling weakly*) I told you they were honest.

EUGENE. I'll give you a hand, Mrs. Atkins.

FRANCES. (*Brightening*) Thank you. Eugene is it?

EUGENE. Eugene Oloff. No brothers. No sisters.

FRANCES. I won't hold that against you. Come on . . .
> *They exit to kitchen.* KAREN *lights a cigarette, gives it to* LESTER, *then lights another for herself.*

TED. From the looks of it, I'd say you two are going steady.

LESTER. Steady? Are we going steady, Kar?

KAREN. I don't know. Are we?
> *Laughs.*
We don't know. Our parents keep pushing us to get married.

LESTER. Yeah. They figure that's the best thing for us. But who needs it?

KAREN. Not unless you want to have children.

LESTER. There are ways to take care of that.

KAREN. (*Smiles knowingly*) Don't we know it.

LESTER. You see, Mr. Atkins, we kids of this generation, we don't play games with one another. We say what we feel. Kary and me have a whatchamacallit, a complete understanding. She does what she wants to do and I do what I want to do.

KAREN. Right.

LESTER. What could be simpler?

TED. Not simpler, no, but maybe it's more complicated, maybe there's something else, something besides getting married for children and . . .

    He's unable to continue.

LESTER. Ahh, that's the old story; we heard it already.

KAREN. Boy, you're way out in left field somewhere, Mr. Atkins. What's wrong with simply being happy and having a good time?

TED. (*Rising, struggling with his thoughts*) Because . . . Because . . .

    Artificial laugh.

I'm not going to say love. Oh, no. You're not going to make me say that. I know you kids. I taught too many years to be taken in . . . But . . . Respect for a woman, a common . . .

    Firmly.

[90

I'll tell you kids something. Now don't laugh and don't try any of your tricks. But . . . I always thought, believed—believed is the word. I always believed that there was nothing more beautiful, more meaningful, than for a man saying—and a woman, too, Karen; it goes both ways—but for a man to say, to all the world, out loud, at the top of his voice, this woman I will be true to, and faithful to, this woman alone, *this* woman, for all the days of my life.

> *A pause.* KAREN *and* LESTER *exchange glances, speak softly, their voices wavering between disdain and sympathy.*

KAREN. It's . . . very pretty.

LESTER. Pretty. Yeah.

KAREN. Very pretty.

TED. (*Almost to himself, his back to them as if ashamed*) I always thought, believed, believed in certain things, certain . . . ideas, let's say. But, I don't know. Ideas like that die, I guess. They die if you hold them too tightly, if there's nothing else.

KAREN. Are you married long, Mr. Atkins?

TED. (*Turning*) Nearly fifteen years.

KAREN. Do you have any other children?

TED. No. No.

LESTER. (*Grinning, to Karen*) A slow worker.

KAREN. He's a young man yet.
> *To Ted.*
Have you decided on any names?

TED. Names?

91]

KAREN. For the baby.

TED. Yes. Yes. We've decided that if it's a boy we'll call him Noah, and if it's a girl . . . Nyreen.

KAREN. They're cute.

LESTER. Noah. That's from the Bible, right, Mr. Atkins?

TED. (*Excitedly*) Right. It took us quite awhile to think them up but we wouldn't want to be caught without a name when the baby . . . Listen. You're confusing me. People do not, I repeat, people do not get married only to have children. Marriage to one person, all your life . . .

LESTER. It sounds like a drag to me.

KAREN. Who needs it?

TED. We all need it. We do! We need it. You can't get it from other people. They don't give anything. You expect so much, you start off and try to get underneath the surface and establish a relationship, an exchange of emotions, a . . .

> *Throws up his hands helplessly; laughs at his own fervor.*

Right. Right you are if you think you are. Do you gamble, Les?

LESTER. Sure.

TED. Bet you a buck it's a boy.

LESTER. Why not? It's fifty-fifty. You got a bet, Mr. Atkins.

> *They shake hands.* EUGENE, *carrying a tray with drinks, and* FRANCES *who carries a single drink, enter.*

FRANCES. (*Singing*) Hail, hail, the gang's all here . . .

[92

EUGENE. (*Continues singing*) Da da da da da da . . .

FRANCES. Help yourselves.

> *Gives drink to* TED.

Here, Ted. It came out A-O.K. if I may say so myself.

TED. How are you feeling?

FRANCES. Fine. Wonderful. Headache's all gone. It's a lucky omen, company our first night here.

TED. Is it? These kids, Fran, they're . . .

FRANCES. I don't want to hear it. Please. Let me enjoy it, whatever it is. I don't care.

> *Moving off.*

How are the drinks?

LESTER. (*Holding up empty glass*) Great, Mrs. Atkins. Any chance of getting seconds?

EUGENE. (*Gulping down drink*) Here, too.

> FRANCES *turns to Ted.*

TED. All right.

KAREN. I'll go with you, Mr. Atkins.

> TED *and* KAREN *take glasses, exit to kitchen.*

EUGENE. You can give me the keys now.

LESTER. I'm not running away. What are you afraid of?

EUGENE. (*To* FRANCES) He's got the keys to my father's car. Shouldn't he give them to me, Mrs. Atkins?

LESTER. I'm going to give them to him. What a character. I just made a bet with your husband, Mrs. Atkins. I say it's going to be a girl.

FRANCES. You say . . . what?

93]

LESTER. I say a girl. Your husband says a boy. We bet a dollar.

FRANCES. (*Slight pause*) He shouldn't have. He always loses.
> *Wildly.*

I have it. Why don't we play some music? We don't want the evening to die out on us. We couldn't allow that. Definitely not. I think it's . . . Here it is.
> *Turns to remove portable radio from box.*

EUGENE. (*Softly to* LESTER) I'll take them from you, you'll see.

LESTER. Go away. You bother me.

FRANCES. I'm going to have to take disciplinary action against everyone who doesn't act like a silly ass. Agreed?

LESTER. Agreed.

FRANCES. Eugene?

EUGENE. Agreed.

FRANCES. And if anyone laughs at seeing a big fat woman dancing, that person is disqualified and a big black cross is marked on his forehead. Agreed?

LESTER and EUGENE. Agreed!

FRANCES. Motion carried. Now let's see . . .
> *She turns on radio.*

LESTER. Don't touch it, Mrs. Atkins. Leave it right there.
> *He "twists" to music.*

Hey, there you go. That's it.

FRANCES. Very very good, Lester.

[94

LESTER. (*Dancing*) It's in my feet. You got it or you don't.
Points to EUGENE.

That man over there, he don't got it; it's sad, sad.

EUGENE. A show-off. A first class show-off.

FRANCES. Our turn, Eugene. Stomach and all. Let's go.

> FRANCES *and* EUGENE *start dancing.* TED *and* KAREN
> *enter, with drinks.* LESTER *and* EUGENE *help them-*
> *selves to the drinks while dancing.* KAREN *immedi-*
> *ately joins in the dance.*

KAREN. Why didn't you wait for us? This is getting to be a real groovy party.

LESTER. I told you. Didn't I tell you?

TED. Fran, it's not wise for you . . .

FRANCES. (*Dancing*) Wise? Who wants to be wise? I'm tired of being wise. I want to be stupid, dumb. If only I could. I'm trying, though. I am trying.

KAREN. (*Dancing around them*) Let's go, Mr. Atkins.

TED. No, I'll . . .

FRANCES. Dance with her, Ted. For once try to be stupid. It's fun. More fun than *Moby Dick*.

KAREN. Don't you know how, Mr. Atkins?

TED. Of course I know how.
> *Starts dancing.*

How's this now? How am I doing?

KAREN. Boy, you're with it; you're really with it. Hey.

LESTER. This is swinging.

KAREN. (*To* EUGENE) And you wanted to go to the movies.

LESTER. Didn't I tell you?

> *The radio suddenly goes dead. Groans of disappointment.*

Hey, what gives?

FRANCES. What happened?

TED. The battery, I guess.

KAREN. Don't you have another one?

TED. Not here, I don't.

FRANCES. What a pity.

EUGENE. Whow, I'm beat.

LESTER. Anyway, I could use a drink now, Mrs. Atkins.

FRANCES. A drink it is, then. All non-drinkers stay in this room, all drinkers . . .

> *Whistles, waves her arm.*

follow me.

> FRANCES *exits to kitchen.* LESTER *and* EUGENE *follow her.* EUGENE *tries to grab the keys out of* LESTER's *pocket.* LESTER *pushes him away.*

LESTER. Hey, cut it out. What a character.

> *They exit to kitchen.*

KAREN. I didn't expect to have such a good time.

TED. Why not? We're not sticks-in-the-mud. Were you all suspended from school?

> *They are both seated.*

KAREN. Nah. Les was lying to you. We quit. When you reach

[96

a certain age you sort of lose interest. I'm looking for a job now.

TED. Anything special?

KAREN. Nah. One job's the same as another, so long as I can make enough for my expenses. Cigarette?

TED. No, thanks.

KAREN. (*Lights cigarette*) The young people of this generation have different ideas, Mr. Atkins. Maybe it's because we've seen too much at a very young age. I don't know. It's unfortunate.

TED. How do you mean? I will take a cigarette on second thought.

KAREN *lights a cigarette, hands it to him.*

KAREN. Well, we don't have respect for grown-ups; which I know can be very harmful. But look what the world is like today. It's utterly ridiculous. Boy. How can you have respect for anyone? It's everybody for himself. Have a good time before the whole works blow up, that's how I feel.

TED. You're not as different as you might think. Most people would agree with you.

KAREN. You wouldn't. I know that. Did you mean all the things you said before?

TED. About marriage?

KAREN. Huhu.

TED. Does it surprise you?

KAREN. It sure does. Especially in this day and age. You mean

97]

you really never even kissed another woman. In fifteen years. Boy, that's something.

TED. (*Laughs ingratiatingly*) I'm not saying I didn't want to . . . at times.

KAREN. I'm weak sexually myself, so it's pretty hard for me to believe. Like, I'm going with Les now but still if I'm out with somebody else, I don't see anything so terrible with, say, kissing him, just to kind of compare it, to see if Les is as hot as he thinks he is.

TED. (*A bit sternly*) That could get you into trouble.

KAREN. What could?

TED. Being indiscriminate that way. And I don't think it's at all fair to the other person who trusts and expects more of you. But I guess those are considerations that don't enter that little head of yours.

KAREN. You sound as if you're mad at me, Mr. Atkins.

TED. (*Rising*) Mad? Well, I am mad, damn it! Listening to you . . . to you spout all that nonsense; the way you behave . . . Obviously your parents didn't see fit to teach you that there's more to human relationships than . . . than swinging your adolescent behind and throwing your body around. Oh, for a young lady, you can do quite well for yourself. I have no doubt about that.

KAREN. I do all right.

TED. I know you do. There are more than enough men who just for the thrill . . . Not because of you, don't think that. It has nothing to do with you. That's where you pay the piper. But . . . Because of their own frustration and sickness . . .

[98

KAREN. I was only talking about a kiss, Mr. Atkins.

TED. A kiss. Of course. What the hell does that mean? I'll tell you what it means. It means that you're no better than a slut, at your age, no better than a common cheap . . .

KAREN. For a kiss? For a simple kiss? Something even like this?

> *She pecks him on the cheek. He stares at her, then grabs her tightly, crushing her to him, and kisses her hard on the mouth. She reciprocates until she can no longer hold her breath, then moves back, panting.*

Boy . . .

> *She smiles;* TED *turns from her.*

You see, you broke your fifteen-year record.

> FRANCES *enters.*

FRANCES. Ted, they're fighting in there. Stop them. They're liable to hurt one another.

> TED *rushes into kitchen.*

FRANCES. Why do they have to fight?

KAREN. They get crazy. I like the rooms you have here, Mrs. Atkins. You should be very happy.

FRANCES. That's kind of you, Karen.

KAREN. The people aren't too bad around here.

FRANCES. We stay pretty much to ourselves.

KAREN. That's what happens when you start having children, I suppose. Mrs. Atkins, I don't want you to get upset now, I'm saying this for your own good, because of the condition you're in and everything: you should watch your husband more closely, he likes to fool around a little.

99]

FRANCES. Are you joking?

KAREN. If I am, the joke's on you.

> *Holding up her hands; laughing to stall* FRANCES' *rising anger.*

Now you don't have to say anything. I wanted you to know. You'll appreciate it in the future. I'm going . . .

> TED, LESTER *and* EUGENE *enter from kitchen. The boys—who had been scuffling rather than fighting —fix their clothes, push back their hair.* KAREN *joins them.*

We're all going.

> *To boys.*

Are we going?

EUGENE. I got the keys.

LESTER. Keep the keys. Keep them. What a character. We're sorry, Mr. Atkins, Mrs. Atkins, for acting up that way. Sometimes you have to let out a little steam.

EUGENE. Yeah. We are sorry. We had a great time.

> *They move toward door.*

KAREN. We did. We really did.

LESTER. Say, Mr. Atkins, you thought I was lying before when I told you about Wallace. Well, you want to know who was involved in O. R. G. I. E. S. with them?

KAREN. Guess who?

LESTER. It was us, who else?

> *They break out in almost grotesque laughter; put on masks.*

KAREN. He's telling you the truth now.

[100

EUGENE. Sometimes he tells the truth.

LESTER. We're off.

EUGENE. Into the night.

KAREN. Trick or treat? Trick or treat?

EUGENE. Good night.

LESTER. Good night, there. Let's go! Let's go! Let's go!
>   *They exit, slamming door.*

TED. Thank God.

FRANCES. What was all that about?

TED. Damn if I know. But if they ever come to the door again, I don't want them in, Fran. Is that clear?

FRANCES. Do you know what she said to me?

TED. Who?

FRANCES. Karen. That girl. She said I should watch you, that you like to play around. I think that's how she put it.

TED. She what?
>   *He runs to door, opens it, looks out, closes it.*
They're gone. I should have kicked them out as soon as they walked in.

FRANCES. What a despicable girl.

TED. Forget them. Let's finish unpacking and go up . . .
>   *The living-room phone rings. They stare at one another.* TED *shakes his head wearily and picks up phone.*
Hello. Who?
>   *A pause; a grin slowly crosses his face.*
Well, I don't . . . It is late . . .

101]

Holds hand over mouthpiece; to FRANCES.

It's Pearce. They want us to join them.

They both become excited, lively. Their eyes shine, they speak in hurried whispers.

FRANCES. Join them where?

TED. Their place. The party they're having.

FRANCES. Now?

TED. What should I tell him?

FRANCES. It is late, but . . .

TED. (*Into phone*) Yes. Yes. I think it would be an excellent chance to meet you and some of the other people.

Laughs a bit too energetically.

I agree with you there. Well, then; we'll be right over. We won't have trouble finding our way. Oh, no.

Laughs.

Right. See you shortly.

Hangs up.

FRANCES. What did he say?

TED. "Hurry over." Now come on; they're waiting.

FRANCES. I can't go like this. I'm not dressed.

TED. You're dressed fine. It'll do for tonight. Where are the handkerchiefs?

Finds one, puts it in his breast pocket.

FRANCES. (*Putting on makeup*) What happened? Why did they change . . .

TED. I don't know.

Shuts kitchen light.

What difference does it make?

FRANCES. Nobody has ever . . .

TED. Come on. Come on.

FRANCES. I'm coming. How do I look?

TED. You look fine. You . . .

> *Turns back to her; suddenly sober, his voice filled with pain.*

Fran.

> *He puts a hand on her shoulder; he can't get himself to do or say more.*

FRANCES. What is it?

TED. (*Burying his pain, forever*) Nothing. Nothing. Didn't I tell you it would work out fine? Didn't I?

FRANCES. You were right. For the first time you were right.

TED. You . . .

> *Stuck for a word.*

character.

> *He shuts living-room light. They exit.*

CURTAIN

REVERBERATIONS

REVERBERATIONS

SCENE:

A cluttered dim basement-laboratory. Rear, right, a short flight of stairs, partially concealed by a sloping wall, leading down into the basement; rear, high on center wall, a paneless window, barred, on a level with the sidewalk outside; left, forward, a large low table on which there is a variety of laboratory equipment; seated, stiffly, dumbly, on the table is a chimpanzee who has several rubber tubes leading from parts of his body and head to an electrical apparatus nearby; crates lie about on the floor and rickety shelves filled with discarded paraphernalia and yellowed note-books are on the walls.

All is darkness. A spotlight is on the steps. Because of the sloping wall we can only see the legs of DOCTOR MAX MILLER *who now appears on the steps, shouting agitatedly.*

MAX. No. No. I'm not hungry. I can't eat. Food. Food. Food. Is that all you can think of? I have my work to do. My work. You said you understood. I thought you understood. But you don't. That's the tragedy. Right there. You say you do, oh, yes, you go right ahead and say you do, you probably think you do, too, but . . .

*He comes down the remaining steps into the base-
ment; he is lost in the darkness. At once* MINA's
*legs appear in the spotlight, her bare legs and a
few inches of her housedress: she wears bulky
white sneakers and sagging red ankle socks. She
is not permitted to go below the bottom step so
that we will see only her legs and her gesturing
hands; three or four times her head will peek out
from behind the stair wall where specified.*

MINA. You haven't had your dinner. You have to eat something. I don't want you to get sick. Your health is important, isn't it? Isn't your health important? You'll get a
headache, you'll see; and then you won't be able to work
and you'll come upstairs and you'll say, "Why didn't you
feed me? Why didn't you give me something to eat?" And
I'll say, "But I tried to, Max. I . . ." But you won't let me
even finish what I'm saying. And you'll say, "You know I
have to eat. Why didn't you force me to eat? What kind
of wife are you?" And I'll have nothing to say to that and
I'll feel miserable, miserable. I won't be able to sleep. I
know I won't. You'll sleep straight through until morning.
But I'll be up all night, feeling miserable and lonely. My
eyes full of tears. Please, Max. Let me bring you down a
plate of cold chicken and potato salad . . .

During the later part of MINA's *lines,* MAX, *his
head buried in a long not-too-clean white laboratory coat, turns on the basement light; he strug-
gles in an effort to pull the white coat over his
head and succeeds in doing so at the end of* MINA's
lines.

[108

MAX. (*Continuing his own incomplete sentence*) . . . You don't. There's the tragedy. You never understood me, Mina. All these years . . . You pretended you understood, and I believed you, I took your word for it, but now I see I made a mistake. It was all a mistake.

He stands on crate, looks about on shelf.

MINA. That isn't true. How can you say that? It's because I disagree with you. Every time I disagree with you, you say I don't understand you. Is that fair? Is it fair? All I want you to do is have your dinner.

Sticks head out.

For my sake, Max. If you don't want cold chicken and potato salad, let me make you a tuna-fish-and-tomato sandwich with French fries or a bowl of hot asparagus soup and a couple of hard-boiled eggs . . .

MAX finds baseball cap, steps down, slaps dust off cap, fixes it jauntily on his head while standing in front of cracked mirror on wall.

MAX. If you understood me, if you really understood me, you wouldn't go on this way. You'd stop and you'd say to yourself, "He wants to work. Food isn't important to him, not when he has his mind on his work. His work. That's what counts. That's what keeps him going. I'll leave him alone now. I'll let him work and exhaust himself and then I'll come down and I'll say, 'Max, would you like to have a cup of black coffee and a little chocolate pudding with sweet cream?'" I'd say, "Oh, that's very thoughtful of you, Mina. I'd appreciate that very much."

Suddenly shouting.

And we wouldn't have to go through this every goddamn time I get ready for work!

He sprinkles talcum powder into a pair of long red rubber gloves then puts them on.

MINA. But I did that last night. I did it. Don't you remember? You said the same thing and I said, "Very well. We'll try it." I waited upstairs, watched television, read a magazine I read twice before, defrosted the refrigerator, and then I came down and I found you asleep on the floor. You wouldn't even think of eating. I called and called. . . . Max, there's something else. I have to tell you. Don't be angry and don't say I don't understand and don't say I'm being silly. But . . . Max, why can't I come down? I mean, all the way down to your workroom? Last night you were on the floor and I was calling you a good ten minutes before you got up. Now what would have happened if you were sick and I stood up here calling you when all the time you needed prompt medical attention? Why do you have to keep me out?

Sticks head out.

And the place is a mess, Max. I can clean it, dust off the shelves, arrange things so that you won't have any trouble getting at them . . .

MAX. (*Removes tubes from chimpanzee*) You don't understand. Good God, you don't, and that's all there is to it. This is my workroom. Where I work. Where every piece and part of it is like an extension of my own body. Would you ask to walk on my body? Would you ask to clean it, to change it? It's private, Mina; intimate, too intimate even for you, and sometimes it's too intimate even for me. Now go up, go upstairs. I have to start. Time, time, it's . . .

MINA. No. Not yet. Please. You've said some things tonight that have hurt me. Deeply. You couldn't have meant them. I must know. Are you sorry you married me, Max? Do you wish you hadn't married me? Has your life been so terrible with me? I must know, Max. Tell me. Please.

MAX. No. No, Mina. No. Don't think it. Never. If I sound impatient, if I sound thoughtless or inconsiderate . . . Time. I don't have the time. There's so much . . . Mina, you know what I want, above everything else; you know what I have to do. You do understand, don't you?

He stands at the foot of steps, looking up at her.

MINA. Of course I understand. I want you to say I understand. Your work, it means as much to me as it does to you. Your achievement, your fulfillment, what else is there for me? I do understand, Max. More than anyone else. Isn't that true? Isn't it?

MAX. Yes. Yes. It is true. It is.

MINA. More than anyone, I understand. And you will do something one day that will be here long after we're gone, and it will be us, we will be here, too.

MAX. We will. I promise. I swear. Granted the time, granted the strength . . . Something. Something right. Something that will help, make brighter. Something that will go on. Why else have I lived?

MINA. What other meaning is there for us?

MAX. We've given everything for it, haven't we?

MINA. If giving everything was the test you would have already succeeded; it would be done and accomplished. But we haven't given up very much, Max. That isn't true. We've kept what is most important, most valuable and precious.

MAX. Each other?

MINA. Each other.

MAX. How good you are.

MINA. Selfish. Selfish.

MAX. Not you. Anyone but you. When I gave up teaching, a salary, a pension, everything, so I could have more time for my work, you never said a word.

MINA. (*Pacing on step*) I was happy. I wanted to.

MAX. When we moved into this house, this rattrap, this old broken-down rattrap, and I said we would probably remain here for the rest of our natural lives . . .

MINA. You're exaggerating. It isn't bad. It's not that old.

MAX. And when we had to decide . . .

MINA. (*Emphatically*) I don't regret it.

MAX. Because there wasn't that much time left to you . . .

MINA. (*Shrilly*) Don't you dare think I regretted it!

MAX. I said then, I said, "No. Not for us. They would cost too much money, they would get in the way, they would take up too much time . . ."

MINA. (*Indifferently*) And you said to me, "But if you want them, if you feel that you have to have them . . ."

MAX. And we agreed, didn't we? I left it up to you but you

said the same thing or you didn't say anything, and we agreed. Didn't we agree?

No answer; shouts.

Mina!

MINA. (*Vehemently*) Yes. Yes. Yes. We agreed. You left it up to me. You said, "But if you want them, if you feel that you have to have them . . ." And I said, "Your work . . ."

MAX. My work. My work.

Hurries to table.

Mina, go upstairs, leave me. I have so much to do . . .

MINA. I'm going, Max. I'm going. Thank you for the very nice things you've said to me tonight. Max . . .

Very quickly.

If you don't want a tuna-fish-and-tomato sandwich with French fries or a bowl of hot asparagus soup and a couple of hard-boiled eggs, I can make you frankfurters and baked beans with a tossed salad and some . . .

MAX. Mina, if I have to . . .

MINA. I'm going. I am. This minute.

Pause.

Is there anything you want me to do upstairs?

No answer.

Max, is there anything you want me to do for you? I'm going up now.

Moving up the steps.

MAX. (*Mumbles while working at table*) You can't keep yourself busy. You still don't know. After all these years . . .

Pause; loudly, in a single breath.

There's a button missing on my gray jacket, there's a hole

113]

in a sock in the bottom drawer of the bureau, and look up
the word "solipsism" for me in the unabridged dictionary
that's holding up the gas range.

MINA. (*Also loudly, yet wearily, coming down*) You told me
to give away the gray jacket months ago. I sewed the sock
in the bottom drawer of the bureau, ironed all your handkerchiefs and solipsism is a philosophical theory that a person can't know anything but his own existence.

> MAX *stops working in exasperation.*

Is that right, Max?

> *Pause; she sits on step, clasps her knees; we can-
> not see her head.*

You know what I was thinking this morning, Max? I was
thinking of the time when we used to walk by the river.
That was before we were married. How beautiful it was.

> MAX *tries to work again, soon stops and listens.*

We used to walk and walk, with our arms around each
other's waist. . . . It seemed as if everything was around
us, as if we were in the very middle of the whole universe
and the clouds and the river and the sun, all of it was where
it was because we were there, in the middle, I mean . . .
Max, I was thinking of the time when we were sitting by
the river and you looked at me and you said, "Mina," and
I said, "I understand you. Why are you afraid? I want the
same things you want." And you said, "Mina," and your
eyes were wet and you were trembling and I took you in
my arms and I said, "Max. Max. Max." And then we talked
for hours and hours,

> *Rises.*

and you said that we had to draw up a contract, that every-

[114

thing had to be crystal-clear so that there'd be no mistakes, no misunderstandings, no recriminations. And I said,

Sticks head out.

"Max, I love you . . ."

MAX. (*Turning to her, excitedly*) And I said, "No. We shouldn't get married." I said, "Mina, this fellow, this book-keeper or whatever he is, he likes you, he'd marry you tomorrow if you said the word. You'd have a normal life. He'd buy you things, he'd spend time with you, he'd take care of you, give you . . ."

Unable to complete thought.

I said, "Mina, you don't know me. You don't know what I'm like, inside; inside that keeps me going, pushes me ahead, it's . . . it's . . ."

MINA. But I said, "I know. I know, Max. There's so much good in you. You want to do things. You want to give some of this goodness to other people."

MAX. (*Strongly*) "I believe in the future," I said.

MINA. "I believe in the future," you said. And I said, "You're not like other men. You're different. And that's the very reason, don't you see . . ."

MAX. You laughed at the idea of signing the contract, though, didn't you? You laughed. You told me I was silly. You said, "Why do we need a contract?" I said, "Because unless you understand what you're letting yourself in for . . ."

MINA. I understood. I did. I said, "Isn't it enough that the two of us will be together? Isn't it enough?"

MAX. You said that. Those were your own words. You . . .

Standing at foot of steps, shouts in anguish.

Mina!

MINA. Yes. Yes. I said it. We agreed. We both agreed. And we didn't need the contract, did we, Max? You're not sorry you married me, are you? Are you sorry you married me?

MAX. No, Mina, no. It was the best thing that could have happened to me. I couldn't have done it alone. Never. I would have given up. Years ago. If not for you . . .

MINA. I did help.

MAX. You helped more than I could have hoped. My work . . .

At once he pulls down cap, runs to table, fills hypodermic needle.

MINA. Your work. I helped in your work. I saw to it that there was no noise, that you had all the time to yourself you could possibly have. And you are doing well in your work. I know you are. You're doing very well in your work.

MAX *lifts chimpanzee's leg, inoculating it in its behind.*

MINA *pauses; timidly.*

Max, I never asked you. But . . . Max.

Sticks head out.

What kind of work are you doing?

MAX. There. There you go again! That's what I get for letting you stay up there!

MINA. (*Very quickly*) It was rhetorical. It was rhetorical. I know what work you're doing. Of course I know. I mean,

how is it progressing? Can you look forward to its conclusion?

MAX. Its conclusion?

> *With hushed excitement, looking about for eaves-
> droppers.*

Mina, if I told you . . . I can feel it. This time it's right.
I'm so close to it, you wouldn't believe it.

MINA. How wonderful!

MAX. Now I'm not putting myself on a limb or anything like
that, but . . . I think . . . I think this is going to be it,
Mina. After all these goddamn years . . . This time I feel
. . . it's going to be right. It's going to be right.

MINA. Max, Max, I'm so happy.

MAX. You know I never looked for any kind of profit from my
work, Mina. You know that.

MINA. (*Indignantly*) Who would dare think such a thing?

MAX. (*Stilted*) And it can be said without any sacrifice to the
truth that I never sought honors or rewards or the cheap
attention that my colleagues run after with greater enthusiasm than they do the interests of their profession.

MINA. I can verify everything.

MAX. But if the community in which I worked and if the
society toward which I have made my small contribution
deem it proper at this time to acknowledge my achieve-
ments, I will with proper humility and gratitude accept
whatever it may be, in the spirit in which it is given, on so
memorial and auspicious an occasion.

> *Removes cap, bows head.*

MINA. (*In same speechmaking tone*) And as the wife of Doctor Max Nathaniel Miller, one who has been privileged, indeed honored, to work by his side through all the years he has devoted to bringing to light whatever it may be, I want to say here and now that he has given to society not only his achievement, not only the child of his genius and his dedication, but he has given to humanity itself his love and the belief in its eternal redemption.

> *Pause; a shade heavier tone.*

Will you please step up here, Doctor Miller.

> *Stiffly and solemnly* MAX *walks up the steps; only his legs are seen on a step lower than* MINA's.

Doctor Miller, today is a day that will not be soon forgotten. What you have done, what you have set as an example to the young people of our nation, will endure wherever men pay tribute to the great, the unselfish and the good. Doctor Miller, congratulations.

MAX. (*Choked voice*) All I can say is . . . thank you.

> *Turns so that he is facing left.*

Thank you all for seeing fit to . . .

MINA. (*Whispering*) Doctor . . .

MAX. . . . to reward me so generously for what I did without any concern for personal profit or tribute . . .

MINA. Doctor . . .

MAX. . . . But with the hope, and with the prayer, yes, with the prayer, that out of my efforts something would be born, something . . .

MINA. Doctor . . .

MAX. (*Whispering to her, annoyed*) What is it?

[118

MINA. (*Very quickly*) They're serving ham-and-eggs, potato salad, chocolate layer cake and . . .

MAX. That does it!

> *Pushing her upstairs.*

Get up there now. Go ahead, get up there. And stay out, do you hear me, Mina? Stay out!

> *Slams door, starts down to table, pulls cap down on brow.*

Don't understand. Never understood. Right from the beginning. I knew it. Talk to her . . . Talk to her . . . Doesn't help. Nothing helps. Nothing . . .

> *He continues mumbling, shaking his head as he works: he puts a glass tube with a funnel end in the left ear of the chimpanzee and another glass tube in its right ear; then he pours a blue liquid down the funnel and it passes through the chimpanzee's head and drips down the other side into a basin. A huge red face appears in the window behind him. HARRY lies full-length on the sidewalk outside the window. Only his head is seen but now and then his hands gesture through the window and he wipes his eyeglasses with a handkerchief. His voice is constrained, dull, almost monotonous wailing.*

HARRY. Pssst. Max. Pssst.

MAX. (*Without turning*) Go away.

HARRY. Mina won't open the basement door. She said I should ask you if it's all right. Max, can I come down? I want to speak to you.

MAX. Tomorrow. Not now. Go away.

HARRY. It's important. I wouldn't bother you if it wasn't important.

> *Pause.*

Max, I can't stay here much longer. I'm on the sidewalk. People are staring at me. It's Dad, Max. The doctor was just over to see him and he's very sick. He's been sick all week. And you didn't phone, you didn't come over. He . . .

> *Raising head; clear voice to someone outside.*

What's that? No, no, I'm all right. I . . .

> *Lowers head; constrained voice.*

Max, I can't stay here. Let me come down and speak to you.

MAX. Go home, Harry.

HARRY. I wouldn't be here if it wasn't for him. I don't care if I never see you again. That's the way you want it, isn't it? But it's for him. He deserves this much from you. You have to see him, Max. You won't believe how much he's changed. He's wasted away to nothing, skin and bones. And his eyes . . . They're popping out of his head and his whole face, it's . . .

MAX. (*Turning to him*) Will you shut up! Shut up! Are you blind? I'm working. I can't be interrupted. Go home, Harry. Leave me alone.

> *Turns to work; removes glass tubes from chimpanzee, takes its temperature, blood pressure, makes notes.*

HARRY. You're not going to hear the end of this, Max. If I

have to stay out here all night I will. I won't go back without you. I promised. I said to him, "Dad, you know how Max is. He doesn't mean anything by it. As soon as I let him know you want to see him . . ." He looked at me with those strange eyes that he's got now and I thought, "Dad. Dad. How is it possible? When was it that you stood like a tower, like a colossus of strength and worldly wisdom . . . When was it that I looked up at you, my mouth half-open, my heart beating with excitement because I was so close to you . . ."

MAX. (*Without turning; fists clenched; shouts*) Harry! Harry!

HARRY. No. No. I'm not going to stop. You're not going to make me stop. He's dying, Max. You know that, don't you? And I sit by his bed and I listen to him. "Where's Max?" he asks. "When is he coming to see me?" You know what hurts. I'm there. I'm with him day and night. But it's you . . . Like always. Why is that? He's living in my home, he's eating my food and benefiting by my attention and sacrifice and . . . Over and over he asks, "Where's Max? Where's Max?" That hurts. That hurts. My wife is working herself sick; my kids have to walk around the house in their stockinged feet; I phone the office, every day, and I tell them I can't come in and . . . "Where's Max?" he asks. "Where's Max?"

MAX. Harry, do me a favor. Please. It won't do any damn good talking about it. Go home. If I get the chance I'll come over and if I don't get the chance . . . My work . . . I have my work to do. My life isn't in him. Not anymore. That's how it is. If you can't understand . . .

HARRY. But his life is in you. He gave you his life. How could you forget? And it was for you . . .

  MAX *paces aimlessly.*

That's what hurts. What he did was for you, not for me. I stood on the side, always stood on the side and watched and said, "All right, let Max go to school. I don't mind getting a job." I said, "Sure, Dad; whatever you think best. I don't need a car now. I can wait." And I didn't mind. That's what hurts. I would have done anything he said, and I would have been glad to do it. I thought we were a family. I thought this is the way families have to be, giving to each other, making sacrifices for each other. When did we stop being a family? When did it happen?

  MAX *slumps wearily into a chair.*

Even after Mother passed away, may she rest in peace, we were close together, closer together than we ever were. Her memory was there, with us, holding us together, saying things to us that nobody else could hear. Dad and I . . . We tried to keep her alive. We spoke about her and we remembered the different times . . . But you. You wouldn't let us. You wouldn't have it. You're the one who buried her, Max, just as you're burying Dad now and just as you want to bury me and everything . . .

MAX. (*Rises, slams cap on table; leaves it there*) You won't leave me alone! Who asked you to come here? Who asked you to sit up there, buzzing in my ear, not letting me work? Tell him whatever you want. Think whatever you want. But . . . Harry. Try to understand. Understand. What I'm doing. What I'm trying to achieve here . . .

HARRY. You haven't been over to see us in six, seven years.

You have two nephews, do you know what they look like? Do you care? But when you needed money, then you came to the office and you said, "Harry, I've got to have some money right away." Did I throw you out? Did I say, "Why don't you come home? Why don't you phone once in awhile so we'll know you're still alive?" No. I said, "How much do you need, Max?"

MAX. And I said, "I need three thousand dollars." And you said, "You must be joking."

HARRY. I said, "I don't have three thousand dollars. I don't have three hundred dollars. Do you know what it costs to keep up a house nowadays, to feed two growing boys, a wife and a father who is your responsibility as much as mine?" I said, "Did you ever give a penny for Dad's support, for his medical bills and all the rest?"

MAX. Then what did I say?

HARRY. You said, and I remember your words exactly, you said, "All right. All right. How much do you want?" And I said, "In view of the high cost of living . . ."

MAX. "Twenty-five dollars a month," you said. Which I sent you every month since that day when I was dumb enough to ask you for three thousand dollars in the first place!

HARRY. And from which day you never got in touch or phoned or so much as said thank you for all I've done for you. Was that nice? Was it, Max? I'm your brother; your flesh and blood. What do you have against me? Why do you avoid me? It isn't natural. My wife makes fun of us. She does. She can't believe it. She says, "What kind of

123]

family do you have anyway? You haven't seen your brother in years and he only lives ten minutes away. It isn't natural," she says. And she's right, Max. That's what hurts. She says, "You only have one brother, one brother and you don't . . ."

MAX. Harry, listen to me. Please.

    Stands under window; pleadingly.

I can't stop what I'm doing now. I can't. I've been at it too long and I'm finally coming near the end, the finish of what I hope will be something . . . You see, Harry, what I want to accomplish, what I'm trying now to successfully conclude . . .

HARRY. I didn't get the chance to tell you, Max. Uncle Eli is sick; he's very sick.

    MAX *stands on crate and nails boards across window.*

Aunt Bertha phoned from the hospital today and she could hardly speak. It was awful. It was terrible. She said, "It's serious, Harry. He's going to leave us. Your Uncle Eli who was so good to you and your brother Max. Where is Max? Why doesn't he phone us once in awhile?" she asked. I didn't know what to say to her. She was hurt. She was terribly hurt. She said, "I never thought Max would turn out to be that kind of person. Here is his uncle, a man who did so much for him, and he doesn't have the common decency and courtesy . . ."

    The window is boarded. MAX *steps down, goes to worktable and replaces rubber tubes to the several parts of the chimpanzee's body and head. He turns a switch on the electrical apparatus.* HARRY *presses his mouth to a small crevice between the boards covering the window.*

Psst. Max. Psst.

No response from MAX.

I'm leaving, Max. I'm not coming back. You'll never see me again. Never. Forget you had a brother, forget you had a father, forget you ever belonged to a family or had anyone who worried about you or cared about you or stayed up nights . . .

MAX. (*Turning*) Go! Go! I want you to go! You're too damn dumb to understand. You don't understand! Go! I don't want to see you again. Do you understand that? None of you. Stay away. Stay away. My work . . . My wife . . . I don't need anyone else or anything else. Go! Go ahead! Go!

HARRY. Your wife? Mina? I saw her. In the kitchen. I gave her a picture I took this week of my two boys. Do you know what she did, Max? Do you know? She cried. She held the picture of my two boys, my sons, my flesh and blood, and she cried. I said, "Mina, why are you crying? What's wrong?" She shook her head. She said, "He said, 'But if you want them, if you feel that you have to have them . . .'"

MAX. You're lying! You're jealous!

HARRY. What did she mean, Max?

MAX. (*Excitedly*) You don't know what you're saying!

HARRY. Want what?

MAX. She said what I said!

HARRY. Feel what?

MAX. She said she didn't want . . . She said . . .

HARRY. (*Moves away from window*) What did she . . .

MAX. (*Runs to foot of stairs; shouts*) Mina! Mina! Mina!
> *The sound of* MINA *walking on top step; her legs
> are not seen.*

He's lying, Mina . . . Tell him he's lying.

MINA. (*Softly, clearly, deliberately cold and emphatic; not
visible*) I hate you. How I hate you.
> *Lights fade.* MAX *turns his eyes to the floor. The
> chimpanzee takes on a crimson phosphorescent
> glow. Darkness except for the fiery-red body of
> the chimpanzee.*

CURTAIN

MEMORIAL DAY

MEMORIAL DAY

SCENE:

A weedy backyard. In the center an old arid water well rising two or three feet above the ground.

It is a hot sunny afternoon, the 30th of May. All is tranquil. Suddenly MR. *and* MRS. LUTZ *enter, left, cross to the well in a burlesque of excited emotions.*

MR. LUTZ. It's over! He said it was over!

MRS. LUTZ. I can't believe it!

MR. LUTZ. What do you mean, you can't believe it? He wouldn't have said it if it wasn't true. We weren't the only people listening.

MRS. LUTZ. That's right. Everybody knows now. It has to be true. It's over! At last it's over!

MR. LUTZ. (*Pause; shaking his head*) I can't believe it. I can't.

MRS. LUTZ. What do you mean, you can't believe it? They never would have allowed him to say it if it wasn't true. Millions of people heard him, all over the country.

MR. LUTZ. That's right. Everybody heard him. It has to be true. It's over!

MRS. LUTZ. He said it was over!

MR. LUTZ. Five years I've waited for this day.

MRS. LUTZ. Five years and three months and two days.
> *They fall to their knees, clasp their hands.*

MR. LUTZ. Our Father who art in heaven . . .

MRS. LUTZ. We thank you for this blessing.
> *They rise.*

MR. LUTZ. You tell him.

MRS. LUTZ. No. You tell him.

MR. LUTZ. You're his mother.

MRS. LUTZ. You're his father.

MR. LUTZ. You're the one . . .

MRS. LUTZ. Who what?

MR. LUTZ. We'll both tell him.
> *They lean over the well, shout into it.*

MR. LUTZ. Peter!

MRS. LUTZ. Are you up, Peter?

MR. LUTZ. Can you hear us, Peter?

MRS. LUTZ. It's over, Peter! It's over, sweetheart!

MR. LUTZ. Now listen to me carefully, Peter. Tie the end of this rope around your waist and give us all the help you can.
> *He jerks rope which is tied to crossbar and already lowered in well.*

MRS. LUTZ. How does he look? How is he?

MR. LUTZ. You know I can't see him.

MRS. LUTZ. (*Clasping hands*) Oh, God, I hope we did the right thing.

[130

MR. LUTZ. We did what was best for the boy.

MRS. LUTZ. His welfare was our only concern.

MR. LUTZ. We couldn't let him go.

MRS. LUTZ. No. That was out of the question.

MR. LUTZ. We had to keep him.

MRS. LUTZ. He was our only child.

MR. LUTZ. And it worked out well. We won, didn't we?

MRS. LUTZ. Yes, we won. And nobody knows; nobody cares.

MR. LUTZ. It's over.

MRS. LUTZ. At last it's over.

MR. LUTZ. Come on, grab this and we'll pull him up.

MRS. LUTZ. Don't hurt yourself, Peter. Be careful.
    The rope gets longer and longer as they tug tenaciously on it, moving far to the left.

MR. LUTZ. You're not pulling hard enough.

MRS. LUTZ. He's gotten so heavy.

MR. LUTZ. I told you to stop throwing apples down at him. It's those damn apples of yours.

MRS. LUTZ. I wanted to make things easier for him. Is that so terrible?

MR. LUTZ. Then pull and stop complaining.

MRS. LUTZ. The rope is burning my hands.

MR. LUTZ. Don't let go whatever you do.

MRS. LUTZ. I can't . . . I . . .

MR. LUTZ. Hold it now. Don't let it . . .

She releases the rope. MR. LUTZ *stumbles into her and also releases the rope; it is sucked down into the well; a dull thud is soon heard. They approach the well, timidly, peer into it.*

MRS. LUTZ. (*Softly*) Peter?

MR. LUTZ. (*Softly*) Boy? Are you all right, Boy?

MRS. LUTZ. (*Remembering*) He can't hear us.

MR. LUTZ. I'll send him down a note.

He takes paper and pencil which dangle on a string at side of well, writes, then puts note in wooden bucket and lowers it into well.

MRS. LUTZ. (*As he writes*) Tell him his mother loves him. Tell him he may have many friends in his life, many sweethearts, but he'll only have one mother . . . and that's me. Tell him the pain I had giving birth to him, tell him the sacrifices I made, tell him the miserable life I had, tell him I'm growing old, tell him he's my only consolation. What did you tell him?

MR. LUTZ. A father's a boy's best friend.

MRS. LUTZ. I thought so. You're up to your old tricks again.

MR. LUTZ. Don't get hysterical.

MRS. LUTZ. I'm not getting hysterical.

MR. LUTZ. We'll have the same arrangement we had before. He stays with you during the even hours and with me during the odd hours. Saturdays he's with you until three, with me until ten. Sunday it's the reverse. Each alternate holiday he spends with me. Even Christmas with you; odd

Christmas with me. Even New Year's with me; odd New Year's with you. Leap year, weekday rules are in effect.

MRS. LUTZ. Very well. It's agreed. But there's to be no brain-washing.

MR. LUTZ. Agreed. Do you have the paper.
        She pulls it out from her blouse.
Let me have it. There's my signature.

MRS. LUTZ. And here's mine.
        He lifts the bucket out of the well.

MRS. LUTZ. How is he? What does he say?

MR. LUTZ. The note's still there. He didn't answer it.

MRS. LUTZ. Why doesn't he write? We haven't heard from him in months. And every morning I send a letter down with his breakfast, begging him to answer me, to give me one word so that I know everything's all right. Do I deserve this kind of treatment from him?

MR. LUTZ. Don't get hysterical.

MRS. LUTZ. I'm not getting hysterical. I'm just asking: what does it mean?

MR. LUTZ. You don't know your own son, lady; you haven't got the least idea what goes on in that boy's head.

MRS. LUTZ. And I suppose you do?

MR. LUTZ. You bet I do. He's down there working, day and night, thinking, planning, using his brains. What was the last thing he asked us to send down to him?

MRS. LUTZ. His teddy bear. He wanted his teddy bear.

MR. LUTZ. The last thing, I said.

133]

MRS. LUTZ. Oh, I remember. A fishing rod.

MR. LUTZ. Right. Now why would someone want a fishing rod down there unless he was experimenting, unless he was doing something scientific with it? That boy's got a head on his shoulders.

MRS. LUTZ. That's exactly what his teacher told me at the graduation exercises. "Mrs. Lutz, your boy's got a head on his shoulders."

MR. LUTZ. He's got what it takes, all right. He's my son.

MRS. LUTZ. And mine!

MR. LUTZ. Don't get hysterical now.

MRS. LUTZ. I'm not getting hysterical.

MR. LUTZ. Come on, let's get him up.
They pull on rope; it gets longer and longer.

MRS. LUTZ. I just wish he had written me more frequently. I deserve that much from him.

MR. LUTZ. You can't keep quiet.

MRS. LUTZ. Stop shouting at me.

MR. LUTZ. Then pull and shut up.

MRS. LUTZ. If it wasn't for Peter, I swear . . .

MR. LUTZ. Pull!

MRS. LUTZ. He's coming. I can feel . . .

MR. LUTZ. Watch it!

MRS. LUTZ. What are you . . .

MR. LUTZ. I can't!

MR. LUTZ *stumbles backwards, sits on ground.*

[134

Most of the rope slides back down well, holding at crossbar.

MRS. LUTZ. Well, whose fault was it now?

MR. LUTZ. (*Rising*) Your fault.

MRS. LUTZ. My fault?

MR. LUTZ. Yes, your fault. If you had held on to the rope the first time we would have had him up by now.

MRS. LUTZ. Go ahead. Blame me.

MR. LUTZ. Who else do you want me to blame?

MRS. LUTZ. Would you mind answering me one question, one simple question? Why, why did you ever marry me?

MR. LUTZ. If I had the answer to that question I'd go to my grave a happy man. Why? Why? Maybe if you had stopped wiggling your behind a minute I would have had the time to sit down and think and say to myself, "No, this isn't the woman for you. Put your hands in your pockets and walk away, now, quickly, before it's too late."

MRS. LUTZ. You say that to me, you, who phoned every night, who wouldn't let me go in until he had ripped the straps off my brassiere, who told my best girl friend Marge Morton that if I didn't marry him he'd jump in the river!

MR. LUTZ. That isn't what I said.

MRS. LUTZ. It isn't?

MR. LUTZ. No, it isn't. I said if you wouldn't marry me *you* could go jump in the river. Get your facts straight, lady.

MRS. LUTZ. My facts are straight, mister. I wanted a divorce. For years and years I've been saying, "Let's get a divorce.

Let's break it up now so that we can salvage something out of this misery."

MR. LUTZ. Sure. And the boy? Would you have given me the boy?

MRS. LUTZ. I'd die first. He's my son. Mine. He belongs . . .
MR. LUTZ *slaps her face.*

MRS. LUTZ. Why did you do that?

MR. LUTZ. I thought you were getting hysterical.

MRS. LUTZ. (*Becoming hysterical*) I was not getting hysterical. You knew I wasn't getting hysterical. I never get hysterical. I don't even know what hysterics are. You did that deliberately, deliberately, deliberately . . .

MR. LUTZ. All right, all right. I made a mistake. Shoot me. Kill me. Crucify me.

MRS. LUTZ. You enjoy hitting me. That has become your chief pleasure.

MR. LUTZ. I have no pleasure, lady. I am in the world to be stepped on, to be mauled, to be eaten, to be ground into dust . . .

MRS. LUTZ. To dream in vain, with nothing happening . . .

MR. LUTZ. That's the one thing we have in common, lady. We both dream, dream of being with someone else, dream of living other lives . . .

MRS. LUTZ. To think that Harry Watson wanted to marry me, that he begged me to marry him, and I said no. Do you know why? Not because you were so handsome or because I believed for a single minute that you would make me happy. I said no because whenever I put on my high-heeled

[136

shoes Harry Watson was shorter than I was, he was at least two inches shorter than I was.

She breaks into painful laughter.

MR. LUTZ. (*Dully*) You should have worn flats.

MRS. LUTZ. (*Recovering*) I should have had my head examined.

MR. LUTZ. Why did you . . .

MRS. LUTZ. It was time. Everyone said it was time.

They walk away from well, move about aimlessly, kneading hands, looking up at the sky, breathing heavily.

MR. LUTZ. I used to look at you and my whole insides would explode. I used to touch you and my throat would become as dry as sandpaper and my legs would start to tremble.

MRS. LUTZ. When I heard that Marge Morton was getting married I became frantic. I was a year older than she was.

MR. LUTZ. I had no self-control when I was a young man.

MRS. LUTZ. I saw everything through the eyes of other people.

MR. LUTZ. I read once, somewhere, that a lot of people marry out of hostility and they stay married to get even with one another.

MRS. LUTZ. I don't know.

MR. LUTZ. I made a good living for my family. No one can say no.

MRS. LUTZ. I tried. I tried as much as any human being could try.

MR. LUTZ. It wasn't my fault.

137]

MRS. LUTZ. You can't blame me.

MR. LUTZ. (*Turning to her; shouting*) Lady, we're getting old!

MRS. LUTZ. Shut up! For God's sake, shut up!

> MR. LUTZ *runs to her, embraces her tightly, brushes back her hair and stares intently at her face; he then releases her as if she had suddenly turned to ice.*

MR. LUTZ. (*In a moment*) Enough. All right. Enough. He's a big boy now; we're all adults. Let him decide.

MR. LUTZ. The one he goes to when he comes up, that's the one who keeps him.

MRS. LUTZ. With no visiting rights.

MR. LUTZ. A complete break.

MRS. LUTZ. Agreed.

MR. LUTZ. Let me have the paper.

> *She gives it to him.*

I'll just add this at the bottom and . . . There's my signature.

MRS. LUTZ. Here's mine.

> MR. LUTZ *tugs at the rope.*

MR. LUTZ. He's got the other end. Don't forget. You stand over there. I'll stand here. He'll decide for himself.

> *They pull on rope.*

MRS. LUTZ. It'll be like a second chance. I have nothing to be afraid of anymore.

MR. LUTZ. A new life. That boy and me, we can go away, start a business somewhere. I told him before he went down,

"Think of a business we can go into, something where I don't have to use my hands, where we can wear white shirts and just sit back and watch the money roll in."

MRS. LUTZ. I'll cook for him and keep his clothes clean . . . He loves me. He has to love me. I'm his mother.

MR. LUTZ. It's over. The war's over.

MRS. LUTZ. At last it's over.

MR. LUTZ. Keep pulling.

MRS. LUTZ. He wanted to enlist. He wanted to go.

MR. LUTZ. But I wouldn't let him.

MRS. LUTZ. I wouldn't let him.

MR. LUTZ. We wouldn't let him. We put our foot down.

MRS. LUTZ. We did what was best for him. We kept him . . . We kept him at home.

MR. LUTZ. Keep pulling.

MRS. LUTZ. He's coming, isn't he?

MR. LUTZ. A little more. Just a little more . . .

> *They pull up a five-foot straw dummy with a grotesquely painted face, wearing a soldier's uniform; it swings on the crossbar. They stare at it a moment, silently, forlornly.* MRS. LUTZ *covers her face and sobs.* MR. LUTZ *puts his arm around her and they slowly exit, left.*

CURTAIN

THE OLD JEW

THE OLD JEW

SCENE:

A poorly furnished room in a tenement building: table, chairs, center; a bureau with a large round mirror on the wall above it, left; a curtained window, rear; an unmade bed, a night table with phone, right; the entrance is in the right wall.

THE OLD JEW *is standing before the mirror, pressing his fingers to his face as if uncertain of its features. He is of medium height, slightly stooped, a man one would guess in his late fifties or early sixties, with a bloodless face, red lips and a bald head that is fearfully bald, tufts of dry hair stick out at the sides.*

As the curtain rises he is chanting a Hebrew prayer or song, loudly, insistently, provoking the knocking on the walls and ceiling that comes from the neighboring rooms. He moves suddenly to the center, as though satisfied with his appearance, and waving his arms exaggeratedly, pacing about, he chants even more loudly, now shouting at the walls and ceiling: he uses nonsense syllables and la-la phrases instead of the Hebrew words, which, in truth, he doesn't know. Finally when the knocking seems unbearable he puts his hands to his ears, runs to the door and throws it open. Almost at once the knocking stops.

THE OLD JEW. (*Breathlessly*) Yes, yes. I know. Forgive me. I am sorry. What else can I . . . You wish to come in? Certainly. Certainly. Please. Be my guest. We have been neighbors, after all, for a good many months now and . . .

> *Hastily putting things in order; wiping dust off the table with a handkerchief.*

You must forgive me. I was not prepared . . . It is so infrequent that anyone . . . A man who lives alone neglects these things and I, unfortunately, as you see, I . . . I live alone. Please. Please, sit down. And forgive me once more.

> *Pulls chair out for each imaginary guest.*

Mrs. Berger, if you will be so kind . . . And, Mr. Thomas. Please. And . . . last but not least, Miss Cino, my next-door neighbor who I must say is as quiet as a bird and from whom I never hear so much as a peep.

> *Uneasy laughter.*

We have seen each other in the hall and in the street so many times and yet . . . We don't speak to one another unless it is a special occasion. Why is that? One of the mysteries of living in this wonderful city of ours, I suppose.

> *Uneasy laughter; raises his hand.*

No, no, Mrs. Berger; not a word. I understand; believe me, I understand. It is not the first time that I have been visited by . . . let us say a delegation of my neighbors. To tell you the truth I was expecting you to drop in long before this, and I can only thank you for your patience and consideration in waiting this long. I have, as you can see, very few things to take with me: the furniture, the curtains, all of that Mr. Miller was kind enough to allow me to use, so I can give you my word that I will be out by the end of the month. No, no, Mr. Thomas; by the end of the month, that is definite. I have caused you people enough inconvenience and . . . how shall I put it? The sooner I go the better it will be for all of us. To you, Miss Cino, I offer my deepest, my humblest apologies. What else can I say? My singing? Why do I sing? That, believe me . . . I don't have the answer. And contrary to what you may think, I don't wait until you turn off your television and go to bed before I begin. No, no, that is not the case, believe me. It is . . . a very difficult thing to explain. Let us say that a Jew sings or he cries, one or the other, and I . . .

Pause; solemnly.

I . . . I am sincerely sorry, Mrs. Berger. I had no idea . . . Yes, it is quite true, quite true. I sometimes . . . But not to excess, not . . . I had hoped . . . I thought it was a private matter. As you see, it is best for all of us that I go, and the sooner the better. But first you must allow me to be a host. A drink, Mr. Thomas? I have some wine, a little rye, perhaps . . . Then coffee? Mrs. Berger, a hot cup of coffee and . . . All right. Say not a word more. I won't insist. But you will stay. On this I will insist. It is so infrequent that I have the opportunity . . . You know better than I do, Miss Cino? Who comes to visit me? Do you ever hear a strange voice coming from this room? Never. Is that not true? Here I stay. Alone. With my own thoughts and my own entertainment. Sometimes I sing; badly, perhaps, but still I sing. And sometimes . . . Well, you are quite right, Mrs. Berger, a hundred percent right; sometimes I walk the floor, back and forth, back and forth, my hands behind me like this . . .

Clasping hands behind him; uneasy laughter.

And . . . as you also know, sometimes, not every night,

Mrs. Berger, you will agree on that . . . my eyes . . . I have little control, they melt down my cheeks and . . . I am quite helpless. Like a baby. I am helpless. But the singing? Ahh, that is another matter. That I confess of my own free will. But do you know what's so remarkable? I sing only Hebrew prayers, the prayers of the Sabbath, prayers that lay in my throat and would choke me, I swear they would choke me, if I did not open my mouth and let them out. Why is that, do you suppose? Mr. Thomas, you're an intelligent man: why is that? I have not gone to the Synagogue in twenty, maybe more than twenty years. I am not a religious man; contrary to what you may think, I am not by any strength of the imagination a religious man, and yet, these prayers that I learned as a child, these prayers that are meaningless to me—oh, yes, quite meaningless, I assure you—they would choke me if I did not let them out. I will be perfectly frank with you, Mr. Thomas. I will speak to you man-to-man. Every Sunday, I give you my word, every Sunday I look out the window and I see you and Mrs. Thomas and your little girls, all dressed in your best clothes, I see you walking down the street to attend services, and I say to myself: There is a religious man, there is a man whom one must respect for his principles. Ahh, believe me, that is no small matter. But tell me, what would you say of a man, a Jew for example, who did not believe in God? Huh? What would you say to him? Is it possible? Is there such a thing? A Godless Jew? What would you say to him? Would you not spit on him? Tear his clothes from his back? Pull his hair and call him the devil himself! Mrs. Berger, I ask you. You yourself are a Jewish woman, a good Jewish woman, I know; maybe one day your boy will be a rabbi or a very important man in the congregation. What would you say? Would you not wish him dead? Would you not curse the mother who gave birth to such a monster, to such an ugly monstrosity? But . . . Wait! Where are you going? Why are you all leaving? No. No. Please. I . . .

Listening; dropping his hands to his sides.

I see. I understand. Yes, yes, of course. You are right, Mrs. Berger; one hundred percent right. Forgive me. All of you. I promise, I give you my word, I will speak so softly you will have to hold your ears to hear me. But. Please. Stay a little while longer. Sit down, Mrs. Berger. What else is there for you to do? Your husband is working, your boy is pasting stamps in his book . . . We have time. Miss Cino, more television? Sit down. Please. We are friends, after all. Friends should spend a little time together, talk, drink, enjoy each other's company. Why not? And when you consider by the end of the month I will be gone . . .

Uneasy laughter.

What have you to lose?

Seated.

The truth of the matter is that you shouldn't take me so serious. I talk, but I mean no harm, believe me. When I first came to this country . . . You didn't think I was born here, did you, Miss Cino?

Laughing.

No, no, I came, let us say, for political reasons. Not that I'm ungrateful. No, no, that isn't the case. But you must understand I came out of necessity, out of . . . How did it happen? Do you really wish to know how it happened, Mr. Thomas? It isn't a long story and . . . You see, I had a premonition when I was a young man. A premonition

147]

. . . I am not sure, frankly, if I am using the correct word, but it was, let us say, a feeling, a warning that was deep inside me. I said to myself: You want to live, leave this country, go someplace else. Plain and simple. No if's or but's about it. The only problem was what I was to do with my family . . . with my young lady friend to whom I was engaged to be married. Where could I put them? In my pocket? Could you put seven people in such a small place?

Forced laughter.

No, that was out of the question. Then where? Not in my luggage. After all, I had no luggage to speak of. Then where? Well, to make it short I said to them: Look, I will go and make arrangements and then you will all come and join me. Plain and simple. No if's or but's about it. My young lady friend . . . Miss Cino, you will understand her feelings. You know, there is a great deal of similarity between the two of you. Many times when I hear you climbing the stairs, coming home from work, I say: It is her, she is coming . . . I listen, quietly: you put your packages on the floor, you open your pocketbook and . . . always you sigh, it is as if you were emptying out your whole soul. Then you take your key and go into your little room and not a peep, not a sound from you until the next morning. Oh, yes, there is television. Every night from nine to ten, no more, no less. No, it is not her, not my young lady friend. She would make noise even in a hospital. And laugh!

Laughter.

I used to say to her: What do you find to . . . to laugh . . . What do you . . .

Pause.

It is not her. No. She is not to be considered anymore. No if's. No but's. I could do nothing for them. And so . . . It is not, I know, an original story. But I will tell you, I am not an original man; no, no, that is perhaps my biggest fault. You see, Mr. Thomas, I find it impossible to forget. Absolutely impossible. Do you know what that means? Do you have any idea what it means to remember, day after day, month after month, year after year . . . And what is the real point of the matter, to remember such a thing when everybody, when the whole world, no longer remembers! Ahh, now we come to it. Now we can understand what a terrible thing this really is. And I am guilty of it. Yes. I confess to the crime. I am absolutely guilty. But what can I do? My friends. You are my friends. Believe me I have nothing but the deepest respect and affection for you. Tell me how not to remember such a thing. That is what I would like to learn. More than anything in the world. To forget, not to remember, the whole business: not my Sheila, not my family, not the others . . . That is over with. It is the past. All right. I am not a stupid man. I have not lost my reason. But . . . everything, the whole business, the idea . . . Ahh, that is what I am trying to say. The idea. How does one forget the idea and yet to continue, to go on as if we are all the same? You, Mrs. Berger, you can't imagine in what high esteem I hold you. No, no, no, I am not flattering you unjustly. You are, after all, raising a family, you are thinking of the future, of buying a house in the country . . . How did you forget? Tell me. How? How is it possible? And you, Mr. Thomas, you go to church every Sunday with your wife and your little girls. Beautiful. It is beautiful to watch. But . . . How? How do you do it? To

149]

what God do you pray? For what do you give Him thanks? Is it for not remembering? Is it . . . No, no, Miss Cino. Please. Not yet. I . . . I am not shouting. No. Really. It is just that these questions interest me greatly and . . . We are talking like friends. That is all. And soon, in another week, in less than a week it is, I will be gone and you will have a new neighbor. Maybe he will be a young man, Miss Cino, and maybe you will . . . well, let us say, you will find many things about him to your liking.

Laughing almost senilely.

You can never tell, Miss Cino. These things happen. Please. Sit down. You know, I have lived in perhaps twenty different apartments since I came to this country and always it's the same story. You would think I would have the intelligence to fill my mouth with rags and take my shoes off when I walk on the floor, but no . . . I must wait until I am asked politely to go someplace else to do my singing and my . . . whatever you wish to call it. But it isn't such a bad life, believe me. I have seen a great many parts of the city and I have met a great many very interesting people. Just think if I had stayed in one place, would I have had such experiences? Never. I don't believe it. I could tell you stories . . . But who wants to listen to my stories? It is a very strange thing, Mr. Thomas, how it is possible for one man to be quiet for so many months and then suddenly to see how everything comes out of him all at once. You know, sometimes when I go downstairs to the street . . . it isn't often I confess but once in a while it happens . . .

Uneasy laughter.

I sometimes look at people and I have the strongest desires, yes the strongest possible desire, to go up to them, to grab them by the coat collar and shout right into their faces all the things that . . . that boil inside me. But, after all, we are civilized human beings—isn't that true, Mrs. Berger? And the police officers in the city, I must tell you, they are always on the job.

Laughing.

Yes, yes, believe me, they are always on the job. But . . . When one remembers, one is compelled to hate; that is perhaps the tragedy. But what can a person do with this hate of his? To use violence we all know is a crime; and to make speeches . . . they will think he is a lunatic and put him away somewhere; that is for certain. There is only one thing permitted such a man. And that is to laugh. Yes, to laugh.

Laughing.

Oh, in private, when he is by himself, of course, he can sing, he can cry, he can do whatever he wishes, provided, we understand, he doesn't disturb his neighbors. But that, after all, is only fair. Why should his neighbors suffer for his . . . for his insanity? What did they do that they should suffer? No, definitely not. But in public, when he's with friends or when he's with strangers . . . In public he must laugh.

Laughing.

Believe me, for such a person life is not a simple matter. He would be doing himself a favor if he locked the door and didn't go down in the street to look for trouble. You can't imagine what thoughts he has in his head, what ideas. If he would be honest with you for one second, just for one second it would be . . . impossible. Absolutely impossible! You, Mr. Thomas, a nice man like you, Mr. Thomas; a man who works hard, who goes to church with his family and who reads all the newspapers to know what is happening in the world, to you he would say the most horrible and insulting things. A hypocrite, he would call you. Yes, yes, a hypocrite and a piece of dead horsemeat that has no feelings and a . . . and a man who is incapable of doing one honest action without looking over his shoulder to make sure that he is followed by the whole country. And you, Mrs. Berger. You, a good Jewish woman, he would call a pig! Worse than a pig! Some fat selfish monster who sticks into her mouth everything she can lay her hands on and who knows when to go tut-tut and oi-oi but who doesn't know what it means to close her mouth for a minute and to feel her heart breaking, yes, yes, to feel and to remember . . . only to remember. And Miss Cino. My Miss Cino. To you he would say nothing. But he would take you by your skinny neck and he would squeeze from you the life that you don't deserve and don't even know what to do with. He would be impossible. Absolutely impossible. He would raise his fist to God Himself and he would shout at the top of his voice . . . He would shout! and shout! and shout! and . . .

Moving to door.

No, Mr. Thomas. Where are you going? You misunderstand.

The phone rings; he turns to it, then turns quickly back to his imaginary guests.

Miss Berger. Please. I am not speaking for myself. No, no.

Phone rings again; he ignores it.

Miss Cino. Listen to me a minute. It is not me. Don't you understand? It is not me who is . . .

> *Phone rings again; he drops his shoulders, walks slowly to the phone, sits on bed; he picks up phone and speaks without foreign inflection.*

Hello.

> *Pause.*

Hi, Jerry. What's up?

> *He pulls the wig off his head, showing a shock of dark hair; he wipes the makeup from his face with a towel, all the while talking on the phone: he is thirty-odd years old.*

I'm all packed. I've been packed for a week. Are you sure it's all right? I mean, there may not be enough room in your place . . .

> *Pause.*

I know. I won't be there more than a couple of weeks. As soon as I get a hold of some loot . . .

> *Pause; lights a cigarette.*

I haven't heard a freaken thing from my agent. Not for months. The crumb. They all stink. They don't care, why should they? No, no. But I did run into this character last night, he's got a theatre down in Williamsburg . . . Who the hell knows where it is but if he can use me, I'm going. They're doing some new things, Molière, I think *Othello*, I don't know.

> *Pause.*

Yeah. Yeah. I'm not bringing Sheila. I told you. No. I'll be there alone. She can go screw herself. It's finished. I mean it.

Pause.

Why don't you come over? I got some wine, Schenley's
. . . We can have a few drinks and then go up . . . All
right. I'll see you tonight. Right. Take care.

*He puts phone down, throws legs onto bed, clasps
hands behind head, stares at ceiling, puffing on
cigarette.*

CURTAIN